SHORT CUTS

INTRODUCTIONS TO FILM STUDIES

THE NEW HOLLYWOOD

FROM BONNIE AND CLYDE TO STAR WARS

PETER KRÄMER

WALLFLOWER

LONDON and NEW YORK

A Wallflower Paperback

First published in Great Britain in 2005 by
Wallflower Press
6a Middleton Place, Langham Street, London W1W 7TE
www.wallflowerpress.co.uk

A catalogue record for this book is available from the British Library

ISBN 1 904764 58 4

Book Design by Rob Bowden Design

Printed in Great Britain by Antony Rowe Ltd, Chippenham, Wiltshire

CONTENTS

ACKNOWLEDGEMENTS

Thanks to Joseph Garncarz, whose exemplary work on German cinema has provided me with a model for the integrated analysis of hit patterns, film industrial developments, shifts in public opinion and generational change. Also thanks to Martin Barker, Mark Jancovich and Jim Russell, who – together with Joseph – provided extensive comments on the manuscript. As always, Sheldon Hall was an invaluable source of information.

Research for this project in American archives was funded by the Arts and Humanities Research Board.

FIGURE 1 *Bonnie and Clyde* (Arthur Penn, 1967)

INTRODUCTION: 1967 AND BEYOND

On 8 December 1967, *Time* magazine's cover announced 'The New Cinema: Violence ... Sex ... Art' with a picture from *Bonnie and Clyde*, a violent, funny and lyrical film about two Depression-era bank robbers; inside, an article entitled 'The Shock of Freedom in Films' declared *Bonnie and Clyde* to be a 'watershed picture, the kind that signals a new style, a new trend' (Kanfer 1971: 331; see also Biskind 1998: 45). The article argued that by building on formal and thematic innovations both in American cinema and, more importantly, in European cinema, and by combining commercial success with critical controversy, *Bonnie and Clyde* demonstrated that Hollywood was undergoing a 'renaissance', a period of great artistic achievement based on 'new freedom' and widespread experimentation (1971: 333). The film provoked a 'battle among movie critics', with Bosley Crowther, a veteran of the *New York Times*, condemning the film, and younger writers like Pauline Kael celebrating it (in the *New Yorker*) (1971: 330). Some critics even battled themselves: '*Newsweek* panned the film, but the following week returned to praise it' (ibid.). According to *Time*, the appearance of films like *Bonnie and Clyde* was made possible by the major studios' unprecedented willingness to open 'doors and checkbooks to innovation-minded producers and directors', many of them unusually young, including 28-year-old Francis Ford Coppola, 'a precocious graduate of the nudie industry' (1971: 331–2). While the magazine was hopeful about the future outcomes of Hollywood's new approach, it also sounded a note of caution: 'For every bold, experimental foray there are bound to be many ambitious failures or cold, calculated imitations' (1971: 333).

Within a few years of the publication of this article, film scholars began to discuss the second half of the 1960s as a period of fundamental change in American film history, tracing the development of the Hollywood renaissance into the 1970s, and variously re-labelling it as 'modern'/'modernist' American cinema or, more commonly, 'New Hollywood' (see Krämer 1998a; for continuing use of the 'renaissance' label see Jacobs 1977 and Man 1994). In the rapidly expanding literature, three critical agreements soon emerged. Firstly, the late 1960s and early 1970s were a golden age in Hollywood history, characterised by a large number of challenging films. Secondly, most of the outstanding films of these years were the work of a small group of young directors, many of them film school graduates like Francis Ford Coppola who had studied at the University of California at Los Angeles (UCLA) before working in exploitation filmmaking. Thirdly, the period of intense formal and thematic innovation which began around 1967 ended in the mid- to late 1970s, with *Jaws* (Steven Spielberg, 1975) or, more often, *Star Wars* (George Lucas, 1977) being selected as markers of another historical turning point.

Confusingly, the term 'New Hollywood' has been applied both to identify a select group of films made from 1967 to the mid-1970s and to refer to this period as a whole. Even more confusingly, the period since the mid-1970s is also frequently called 'New Hollywood'. To avoid such confusion, I only use the term to refer to the period 1967–76 in American film history (that is all American films, the film industry and the wider film culture during these years).

While publications about the New Hollywood and its key films and directors have appeared at an impressive rate since the 1970s, from the late 1990s onwards there has been an explosion of interest. In 1998, Peter Biskind's *Easy Riders, Raging Bulls: How the Sex-Drugs-and-Rock 'n' Roll Generation Saved Hollywood* demonstrated that there was a large audience for an in-depth account of the lives and films of some of the key Hollywood personalities of the late 1960s and 1970s (in 2003 a documentary with the same title was released). In 2000 and 2001, volumes on the 1960s and 1970s were published in Scribner's authoritative 'History of the American Cinema' series, providing future scholars with an important reference point (Cook 2000, Monaco 2001). The year 2000 saw the publication of the third edition of Robert Kolker's by then classic study of key Hollywood directors since the 1960s entitled *A Cinema of Loneliness: Penn, Stone,*

Kubrick, Scorsese, Spielberg, Altman (the first edition had been published with a slightly different line-up of directors in 1980). Three years later, Ryan Gilbey's *It Don't Worry Me: Nashville, Jaws, Star Wars and Beyond* discussed ten essential directors of the 1970s (including Coppola, George Lucas, Terrence Malick, Brian De Palma, Woody Allen and Jonathan Demme as well as most of the directors in Kolker's line-up). Furthermore, Peter Lev (2000) analysed some of the decade's most important cycles, ranging from hippie films to blaxploitation, and Stephen Paul Miller (1999) offered readings of key 1970s films in relation to American politics and culture (for earlier examples of this kind of work see Bernardoni 1991; Ryan & Kellner 1988: chs. 1–6; and Ray 1985: chs. 8–10). Several New Hollywood films have also recently been the subject of volumes in the British Film Institute's Modern Classics series and in the Cambridge Film Handbooks series. Tom Stempel (2001) examined people's memories of cinemagoing during the last few decades, including several chapters on the 1960s and 1970s, while Geoff King (2002), Michael Allen (2003) and also, somewhat idiosyncratically, Richard W. Haines (2003) have offered comprehensive accounts of American cinema since the 1960s, situating the New Hollywood of 1967–76 in broader film historical contexts.

Similarly, both Jon Lewis (1998) and Steve Neale and Murray Smith (1998) published important edited collections on American cinema since the 1960s, including essays on key aesthetic, ideological, industrial and technological developments of the 1960s and 1970s. In addition, more than half of J. Hoberman's *The Dream Life: Movies, Media, and the Mythology of the Sixties* (2003), a political discussion of a range of important films and filmmakers, dealt with the period 1967–76, as did much of Robin Wood's classic study *Hollywood From Vietnam to Reagan* (first published in 1986), an extended edition of which came out in 2003. Last but not least, Thomas Elsaesser, Alexander Horwath and Noel King's edited collection *The Last Great American Picture Show: New Hollywood Cinema in the 1970s* (2004) contained survey essays as well as detailed case studies of films and filmmakers, and was produced in conjunction with two major retrospectives of American cinema from 1967 to 1976, the first at the Viennale, Vienna's international film festival, in 1995, and the second at the Berlin Film Festival in 2004.

In this book, I discuss the films of the New Hollywood as products of their time, locating the work of filmmakers (by which I mean not only directors but also producers, scriptwriters, actors and so on) in the context of changes in the film industry, in its audiences and, more broadly, in American society in the 1960s and 1970s. Unlike most previous studies of the New Hollywood, mine is going to deal primarily with the period's biggest hits (for a similar methodological approach see Garncarz 1994 and 1996). Some of these hits were made by the great directors usually associated with the New Hollywood, while the majority were not. The main reason for studying hits is that they were enormously important both for the film industry and for audiences; they generated a substantial portion of Hollywood's income and were seen by the largest numbers of people, many of whom watched them repeatedly.

In examining hit movies, I look for what they have in common with each other. Some of these commonalities distinguish the hits of the New Hollywood from Hollywood's big hits in the years before 1967 and after 1976. In the conclusion I comment on new patterns of success from 1977 onwards, which are most closely associated with the science fiction and adventure films made by George Lucas and Steven Spielberg, especially *Star Wars*. In the main body of this book, however, I compare New Hollywood successes with hits in preceding decades. This comparison throws the distinctive qualities of the New Hollywood into sharp relief and confirms that American film culture underwent a dramatic re-orientation in the course of the 1960s.

It is important to note that the present study of this re-orientation deals only with thematic currents, rather than with formal and stylistic developments. Elsewhere (Krämer 1998a) I have outlined the long-standing and ongoing critical debates about aesthetic changes in Hollywood from the 1940s to the present, with a particular focus on the 1960s and 1970s. No doubt there is important work still to be done in this area. However, in the following chapters I concentrate on filmic content.

Chapter one identifies a group of fourteen breakaway hits for the period 1967–76 and demonstrates the central role they played in American film culture, in terms of their economic importance, their audience reach, their tie-ins with best-selling books, records and Broadway shows, their decisive impact on future film production and hit patterns, their status as audience favorites as well as their high critical standing both in the press and in the film industry itself. The distinctive thematic features of these New Hollywood superhits are then examined by way of comparison with the superhits of the preceding era (1949–66), most of which had originally been addressed to family audiences and received a so-called 'roadshow' release.

Chapters two and three offer an explanation for the shift in hit patterns from the Roadshow Era to the New Hollywood. The first of these two chapters outlines several interconnected changes in film production (notably the rising output of taboo-breaking movies in the late 1960s and the eventual replacement of traditional family roadshows in the early 1970s) and in movie audiences (notably the increasing importance and specific interests of young people), which together determined changing hit patterns. The third chapter aims to understand why film production and movie audiences changed. It does so by examining shifts in public opinion (characterised by both liberalisation and polarisation) and the restructuring of the film industry (with closer corporate links to other media and the rise of new generations of filmmakers).

1 SUPERHITS OF THE NEW HOLLYWOOD AND THE ROADSHOW ERA

In December 1967 *Time* magazine noted that *Bonnie and Clyde* was a 'popular success' (Kanfer 1971: 333). In fact, while the film was widely debated in the press and perceived as a cultural phenomenon, the box office takings of its first release in August 1967 were limited, and it was nowhere to be seen on *Variety*'s end-of-year list of the twenty top-grossing movies of 1967 (Steinberg 1980: 25). Only when the strong media response motivated Warner Bros. to re-release the film in February 1968 did it become a major hit with total rentals of $23m (see Biskind 1998: 38–41, 45–6). Taking the 1968 earnings into account, *Bonnie and Clyde* appears at no. 4 in a revised list of the top-grossing movies released in 1967 (see appendix 1). However, the breakaway hit of 1967 was what *Time* described as 'an alternately comic and graphic close-up of a 19-year-old boy whose central fantasies come terrifyingly true' (Kanfer 1971: 324). Released late in the year, *The Graduate*, went on to earn rentals of $44m, mostly in 1968.

Let us try to put this figure into perspective. 'Rentals' refers to the money that cinemas pay to distributors for film hire; rentals usually amount to between 40 per cent and 60 per cent of the box office gross, that is the money paid by cinemagoers for tickets. Box office takings for *The Graduate* were $105m (*Variety* 2000: 65). In 1968, the year *The Graduate* made most of its money, total box office revenues from all films in all movie theatres in the US were $1,045m (Finler 2003: 377). Thus, *The Graduate* took in every tenth dollar spent on movie tickets in 1968. In that year, the major studios (Columbia, Fox, MGM, Paramount, United Artists, Universal and Warner

Bros.) released 177 films, including both US-produced films and imports; independent distributors, such as Embassy, the company behind *The Graduate*, released another 277 films (Finler 2003: 366–7). In addition to this total of 454 films, there were many films like *The Graduate* which had been released in 1967 (or even earlier) but were still in circulation in 1968. *The Graduate*, then, prevailed against enormous competition.

Another way of appreciating the enormity of the film's success is to calculate the number of tickets it sold. The average ticket price in 1968 was $1.31, which means that 80m tickets were sold for the movie. This was equivalent to 40 per cent of the total American population (Wattenberg 1976: 8). However, this does not mean that four out of ten Americans saw the film, because observers at the time noted that many people watched the film several times (Alpert 1971: 405).

It was also noted that the audience for *The Graduate* was predominantly a young one. This is not surprising since young people were the main cinema-ticket buyers in the late 1960s. A 1967 survey for the film industry's main trade organisation, the Motion Picture Association of America (MPAA), revealed that 'half of the United States population 16 years and older almost never goes to the movies' (Warga 1968: 1). Those who did attend frequently (that is once a month or more) were mostly young; only 18 per cent of the total sample, but 78 per cent of 16–20-year-olds were frequent cinemagoers. Out of all the tickets purchased by those aged 16 and older, almost 30 per cent were bought by 16–20-year-olds, 18 per cent by 21–24-year-olds and 10 per cent by 25–29-year-olds; hence 58 per cent of tickets were bought by those aged 16–30. What is more, youth and older adults had strongly divergent opinions about movies: 'Objections to the fact that movies deal more explicitly with sex split the population at about 30 years of age'; people under 30 were largely in favour of such explicit treatment, those over 30 mostly were not (Warga 1968: 14). Thus a film like *The Graduate*, with its (by the standards of the time) fairly explicit depiction of the affair between a young man and an older, married woman, was dividing the nation, with youth clearly on its side and older generations largely opposed. (A similar division of public opinion was noted with respect to violent films such as *Bonnie and Clyde*.)

The above discussion suggests not only that *The Graduate* was mostly seen by young people, but also that most young people saw *The Graduate*, often several times. The film's impact on American youth does not end here. Its soundtrack, recorded by Simon and Garfunkel, was the second biggest-selling album of 1968, and 'Mrs Robinson' (the name of the film's older woman) one of the ten top-selling singles of the year (*People* 2000: 220, 224). It would seem, then, that *The Graduate* was at the very heart of American youth culture in 1968. In this chapter, I shall first discuss 14 films from 1967 to 1976 which achieved a similar level of success. I shall then identify the 14 biggest hits from 1949 to 1966, and compare them to the ones from 1967–76.

The New Hollywood Top 14, 1967–76

Almost every year from 1967 to 1976 saw the release of one or more breakaway hits whose success was of a similar magnitude to that of *The Graduate* (see appendix 1):

1967   *The Graduate* (with rentals of $44m and a box office gross of $105m)
1969   *Butch Cassidy and the Sundance Kid* ($46m/$102m)
1970   *Love Story* ($49m/$106m) and *Airport* ($45m/c.$80m)
1972   *The Godfather* ($87m/$135m) and *The Poseidon Adventure* ($42m/$85m)
1973   *The Exorcist* ($89m/$165m), *The Sting* ($78m/$156m) and *American Graffiti* ($55m/$115m)
1974   *The Towering Inferno* ($49m/$116m) and *Blazing Saddles* ($48m/$120m)
1975   *Jaws* ($130m/$260m) and *One Few Over the Cuckoo's Nest* ($60m/$112m)
1976   *Rocky* ($57m/$117m)

Due to inflation, the figures from the late 1960s are not directly comparable to those of the mid-1970s; the average ticket price rose from $1.20 in 1967 to $2.13 in 1976 (Finler 2003: 379). Nevertheless, even an inflation-adjusted tabulation lists the above fourteen films as the greatest hits of the period 1967–76 (see appendix 2).

This section deals with the commercial, cultural and critical status of these superhits, which, for simplicity's sake, I will refer to as 'the New Hollywood Top 14'. As we will see, these fourteen films are closely connected to trends among the annual top ten, in so far as their breakaway success exerted a strong influence on future hit patterns, while this success in turn derived partly from already existing trends. Among other things, this means that the results of my analysis of superhits would not change substantially if I enlarged the group of films under investigation from 14 to 20 or 30.

The market share of each of the Top 14 ranges from 5 per cent to 12 per cent. In 1976, for example, *Rocky*'s box office earnings of $117m made up 6 per cent of all the money ($1,994m) spent on the purchase of movie tickets during that year (Finler 2003: 377). The strongest concentration of ticket purchases on superhits occured in 1973. Between them, *The Exorcist*, *The Sting* and *American Graffiti* earned $436m, which was 29 per cent of all box office takings in 1973; this means that almost three out of every ten cinema tickets bought in 1973 were purchased for one of these films.

Furthermore, like *The Graduate*, all of the Top 14 reached a substantial portion of the American population. For example, with an average ticket price of $2.13 in 1976 (Finler 2003: 379), *Rocky*'s box office take of $117m was equivalent to 55m tickets; this in turn was equivalent to about a quarter of the American population at the time. With a gross of $260m and an average ticket price of $2.05 in 1975, *Jaws* sold 127m tickets, which was equivalent to an astonishing 60 per cent of the American population. While this does not mean that three out of five Americans actually saw the film at the cinema (because no doubt many saw it several times), the ability of superhits such as *Jaws* to lure large segments of the American population into cinemas is impressive.

Many of the Top 14 also had spectacular ratings when they were shown on television. The *Love Story* broadcast on 1 October 1972 had a 42 rating, that is, 42 per cent of all households were tuned in (Steinberg 1980: 32). Except for the *Bob Hope Christmas Show* of 1970 and the final episode of *The Fugitive* in 1967, *Love Story* was the most popular television programme in American history up to this point (*People* 2000: 162). The record audience for *Love Story* was matched by *Airport* when it was broadcast a year later. Furthermore, *The Godfather* (shown in 1974), *The Poseidon Adventure* (1974), *Jaws* (1979), *Rocky* (1979), *Butch Cassidy and the Sundance Kid* (1976), *The Sting* (1978) and *The Graduate* (1973) all had ratings in excess of 30 (Steinberg 1980: 31–3). As of 1979, five of the Top 14 were among the ten top-rated theatrical movies ever shown on television, and the only made-for-TV movie that outdid them was the mini-series *Roots* (1977) (Steinberg 1980: 31–2; *People* 2000: 162).

As with *The Graduate*, there are yet more ways in which these films resonated across American culture. The following soundtracks were placed in the top ten of *Billboard*'s annual album charts: *Butch Cassidy and the Sundance Kid* (no. 8 in 1970), *American Graffiti* (no. 6 in 1974) and *The Sting* (no. 9 in 1974) (*People* 2000: 224). There also were more singles taken from the soundtracks of movie hits. 'Raindrops Keep Fallin' on My Head' from *Butch Cassidy and the Sundance Kid*, for example, was the fourth best-selling single of 1970 (*People* 2000: 220).

Another indicator of the resonance the Top 14 had across American culture is the fact that nine of the fourteen were based on recently published, often very popular novels. The films drew on the popularity of these novels, which in turn profited from the popularity of the films. This mutually beneficial relationship resulted in increased sales both of cinema tickets and of books (in a similar fashion, ticket sales and soundtrack as well as singles sales were also mutually reinforcing). There was probably only a limited impact on ticket sales figures in the case of *The Graduate* (the original novel by Charles Webb was published in 1963), *One Flew Over the Cuckoo's Nest* (Ken Kesey, 1962), *The Poseidon Adventure* (Paul Gallico, 1969) and *The Towering Inferno* (based on two books, Richard Martin Stern's *The Tower*, 1973, and Thomas N. Scortia and Frank M. Robinson's *The Glass Inferno*, 1974). However, the other five films profited hugely from the best-seller status of the novels they were based upon. Arthur Hailey's *Airport* had been the best-selling fiction hardback of 1968; Mario Puzo's *The Godfather* had been no. 2 in 1969, Erich Segal's *Love Story* no. 1 in 1970, William Peter Blatty's *The Exorcist* no. 2 in 1971 and Peter Benchley's *Jaws* no. 3 in 1974. Once the films had come out, all of these novels sold millions more copies in paperback, usually with cover designs that tied them in with the movies. Indeed, four of these novels soon made it into the top ranks of the list of best-selling books in the US between 1895 and 1975. With 12.1m copies sold in hardback and paperback, *The Godfather* was the highest-ranked fiction title on this list at no. 6, closely followed by *The Exorcist* (11.7m copies, no. 7), *Love Story* (9.9m, no. 12) and *Jaws* (9.5m, no. 14); *Airport* sold 5.5m copies (see Hackett & Burke 1977: 10–11).

In various ways, then, the Top 14 were at the centre of American film culture between the late 1960s and the mid-1970s. They generated a substantial share of the film industry's income from ticket sales, each attracting between a quarter and half of the American population to its screenings. The majority of these films were among the top-rated movies ever shown on television, reaching 30–40 per cent of all American households this way. Most of the breakaway hits were tied-in either with a best-selling soundtrack or a best-selling novel.

In this way the extraordinary status of breakaway hits can be quantified. Less quantifiable is the equally important impact each of these films had on future film production, and also on the future film selections made by movie audiences. It is reasonable to assume that the film industry tries to copy breakaway hits, either by imitating them wholesale or by extracting and combining key elements from several hits (see Altman 1999: 38). Similarly, most cinemagoers probably try to find films which can be expected to replicate the enjoyment they experienced with previous films. Since the success of films depends to a large extent on positive word-of-mouth (see De Vany 2004), the biggest hits are the films that were enjoyed by most people and that therefore provide the model for their future film choices.

It is to be expected, then, that every big hit sparks off a wide range of imitations and combinations, many of which will in turn become big hits. This effect can be observed when examining the annual top ten lists of the period (see appendix 1). To begin with, the enormous success of *The Graduate* in 1967/68 established Dustin Hoffman as a new superstar, who was ranked from 1969 to 1972 and then again in 1976 as one of the ten top box office attractions by American exhibitors in the annual star poll conducted by Quigley Publications (Quigley's star rankings often registered box office hits with a one-year delay; see Steinberg 1980: 60–1). Although he played diverse roles in diverse films rather than replicating the model of *The Graduate*, Hoffman's presence was perceived to be a key factor in the success of *Midnight Cowboy* (the third highest-grossing film of 1969), *Little Big Man* (6th/1970), *Papillon* (4th/1973) and *All the President's Men* (5th/1976) as well as films outside the annual top ten.

Another element of *The Graduate* which became central to later hits was its pop soundtrack. During the preceding decade, the only best-selling albums generated by Hollywood's superhits featured showtunes or orchestral scores, whereas several smaller hits, mostly star vehicles for Elvis Presley and the Beatles, were associated with top-selling rock and pop records (see appendix 3 as well as the singles and album charts in *People* 2000: 218–9, 223; see also Smith 1998, and Denisoff & Romanowski 1991). After *The Graduate, a wide range of* pop, rock and blues songs were featured in, among many other hit movies, *Butch Cassidy and the Sundance Kid* (1st/1969), *Midnight Cowboy* (3rd/1969), *Easy Rider* (4th/1969; the film's soundtrack became the seventh best-selling album of 1970) and *American Graffiti* (3rd/1973) as well as the documentary *Woodstock* (5th/1970) and the musicals *Lady Sings the Blues* (10th/1972; the no. 5 album of 1973), *Tommy* (10th/1975) and *A Star is Born* (2nd/1976; the no. 3 album of 1977) (*People* 2000: 224).

More generally, it is likely that the enormous success of *The Graduate* encouraged both audiences and filmmakers to shift their attention away from the female protagonists as well as the mostly past and foreign settings so dominant in mid-1960s superhits (most notably in *Cleopatra*, *My Fair Lady*, *Mary Poppins* and *The Sound of Music*; see appendix 3) towards male protagonists and the contemporary American scene. There is also the possible influence of the film's ambiguous ending, in which the lovers are finally united but seem unsure about each other and their future, on later hits emphasising the problems and failure of romantic relationships, such as *Funny Girl* (the highest-grossing film of 1968), *Goodbye, Columbus* (10th/1969), *Carnal Knowledge* (8th/1971), *The Last Picture Show* (9th/1971), *Cabaret* (6th/1972), *The Way We Were* (5th/1973), *Shampoo* (3rd/1975) and *A Star is Born* (2nd/1976).

By combining the outlaw antics of *Bonnie and Clyde* (5th/1967) with the comedy of *The Odd Couple* (3rd/1968), in 1969 *Butch Cassidy and the Sundance Kid*, together with *Midnight Cowbody* and *Easy Rider*, turned the often comic and in places very touching interaction between two male friends (in the above cases mostly on the wrong side of the law) into a successful formula for Hollywood hits. The most direct imitation, once again featuring Paul Newman and Robert Redford as sympathetic criminals, was *The Sting* (2nd/1973), yet similar 'buddy' relationships could also be found, for example, between two policemen in *The French Connection* (3rd/1971), between two prisoners (played by Steve McQueen and Dustin Hoffman) in *Papillon* (4th/1973) and between two reporters (Redford and Hoffman) in *All the President's Men* (5th/1976). Further variations include the black sheriff and his white deputy in *Blazing Saddles* (2nd/1974), and the groups of friends in *M*A*S*H* (3rd/1970) and *Catch-22* (9th/1970) as

FIGURE 2 *Butch Cassidy and the Sundance Kid* (George Roy Hill, 1969)

well as *Deliverance* (4th/1972), also the men who grow to be friends in *Jaws* (1st/1975) and *One Flew Over the Cuckoo's Nest* (2nd/1975). Many other hit films from the period – ranging from *The Godfather* to disaster movies and cop films – focused on friendships or partnerships between men. This was not unprecedented but it became more pronounced than ever before in the years following *Butch Cassidy and the Sundance Kid*. The influence of this pattern may even be seen in the central relationships between a grown man and a tomboyish girl in *True Grit* (8th/1969), *Paper Moon* (8th/1973) and *The Bad News Bears* (7th/1976), and between 'Dirty Harry' and his female partner in *The Enforcer* (8th/1976).

Replicating the abrupt violent ending of *Bonnie and Clyde*, in which the two protagonists are massacred, *Butch Cassidy and the Sundance Kid*, together with *Easy Rider*, also confirmed the violent death of one or more of the protagonists as a key ingredient for many movie hits during this period, including *The Poseidon Adventure* (2nd/1972), *The Exorcist* (1st/1973), *Last Tango in Paris* (7th/1973), *Earthquake* (4th/1974) and *One Flew Over the Cuckoo's Nest* (2nd/1975). Other hits featured protagonists dying from illnesses, including *Midnight Cowboy* (3rd/1969), *Love Story* (1st/1970) and *Lady Sings the Blues* (10th/1972). While the death of protagonists was also a staple of hits before the late 1960s, *Butch Cassidy and the Sundance Kid* and other New Hollywood successes tended to foreground its meaninglessness. Earlier hits such as *The Ten Commandments* provided meaning for the deaths of protagonists by emphasising that they had led a full life and death was its natural conclusion. Furthermore, religious films such as *The Ten Commandments* and *The Robe* emphasised that a glorious afterlife awaited those who died. If protagonists met an early, violent death, it was mostly because they died in the line of duty, perhaps even sacrificed themselves for a good cause (as in many war films). Death might also be the only way for lovers to be united, as in *Cleopatra*, and even in non-religious films it was not an absolute end, because the dead would live on in their children (as they do in *Doctor Zhivago*). While such comforting depictions of death did not disappear altogether, *Butch Cassidy and the Sundance Kid* suggested that abrupt and pointless death was not, as one might assume, putting audiences off, but instead seemed to appeal to them.

Moving on to *Airport* in 1970, we can see that one of the elements that made the film such an enormous hit in 1970 was the fact that it featured two near-disasters (an on-board explosion which almost destroys a packed airplane and an obstacle blocking the plane's emergency landing). Filmmakers extracted this element, exaggerated it and moved it to the centre of subsequent productions (see Roddick 1980). In addition to several less successful films, this resulted in four big hits over the next four years: *The Poseidon Adventure* (2nd/1972, set on a sinking ocean liner), *The Towering Inferno* (1st/1974, set in a burning skyscraper), *Earthquake* (4th/1974, set in an earthquake-ravished city) and *Airport 1975* (7th/1974, a return to the original setting); due to the large-scale destruction brought to New York by the eponymous monster, *King Kong* (3rd/1976) could also be added to this list.

Furthermore, *Airport*'s focus on the day-to-day operations of a large-scale organisation, on the place of key individuals within that organisation and on their professional skills became an important model for numerous subsequent hits. Before the late 1960s, this 'procedural' focus could mainly be found in certain war movies and in the James Bond series, in science fiction and crime films (indeed, I have borrowed the term 'procedural' from writings on crime fiction; the police procedural has been one of the dominant trends in crime novels and crime movies since the 1940s; see Wilson 2000: chs. 2–3). In the wake of *Airport*'s breakaway success an emphasis on organisational hierarchies and professional procedures could be found in many top-ten hits (including several of the Top 14), ranging from subsequent disaster movies and further Bond, crime and war films to movies as diverse as the musical *A Star is Born*, which dealt with the music industry, and the newspaper drama *All the President's Men*. Furthermore, several hits highlighted the procedural dimension of activities taking place outside organisational frameworks, for example river rafting in *Deliverance* (4th/1972), survival in the wilderness in *Jeremiah Johnson* (5th/1972), confidence tricks in *Paper Moon* (8th/1973) and maverick science in *Young Frankenstein* (3rd/1974).

Also in 1970, the success of *Love Story*, with its cross-class romance between the scion of an old WASP family and the daughter of an Italian immigrant, confirmed an important trend already under way since 1967 – the centrality of ethnic American characters (see Erens 1984: 262–78). Previously, this had been a feature mainly of Second World War combat movies with their ethnically-mixed platoons (see Basinger 1986), but in the late 1960s hit movies, including many of the Top 14, across a range of genres came to be populated with Americans from ethnic minorities. Italian-American characters could be found in leading roles in films ranging from *Midnight Cowboy* (3rd/1969) to *The Godfather Part II* (6th/1974) and Jewish-Americans in films such as *Goodbye, Columbus* (10th/1969). Furthermore, actors who through the publicity surrounding their off-screen lives and also, to some extent, through their looks were identified as Jewish-American or Italian-American (even if they did not play ethnically-marked characters in all of their films) rose to the top from 1967 onwards (see Levy 1989: 39–41, and Jarvie 1990). In addition to Dustin Hoffman, these included Barbra Streisand, who starred in *Funny Girl* (1st/1968), *Hello, Dolly!* (5th/1969), *The Owl and the Pussycat* (10th/1970), *What's Up, Doc?* (3rd/1972), *The Way We Were* (5th/1973), *Funny Lady* (8th/1975) and *A Star is Born* (2nd/1976) as well as several lesser hits, and was listed as one of Quigley's top-ten box office attractions in seven out of nine years from 1969 to 1977 (Steinberg 1980: 60–1). It is worth mentioning that Streisand was also one of the most successful recording artists of the 1960s and 1970s, with, for example, three albums in the top ten for 1964 and one each in 1966, 1969 (the soundtrack for *Funny Girl*) and 1977 (*A Star is Born*), as well as the best-selling single of 1974 ('The Way We Were') and the fourth best-selling single of 1977 ('Love Theme from *A Star is Born*') (*People* 2000: 220, 223–4).

Al Pacino's hits included the *Godfather* movies and *Dog Day Afternoon* (4th/1974), and he made Quigley's top ten from 1974 to 1977. Walter Matthau starred in *The Odd Couple* (3rd/1968), *Hello, Dolly!* (5th/1969), *Cactus Flower* (9th/1969) and *The Bad News Bears* (7th/1976), and made Quigley's top ten in 1971. Gene Wilder starred in *Blazing Saddles* (2nd/1974), *Young Frankenstein* (3rd/1974) and *Silver Streak* (4th/1976) but was not ranked in the top ten by American exhibitors, whereas both Mel Brooks (in 1976–77) and Woody Allen (1975–77) made Quigley's list, although their star vehicles did not feature in the annual top ten (Brooks only had a supporting role in *Blazing Saddles*). Most of these distinctly ethnic actors started their film careers after 1966, and none was considered a major box office attraction before *The Graduate* made Hoffman a star.

Thus, by offering new models for future film production and for the audience's future film choices or by enhancing existing trends, individual breakaway hits such as *The Graduate*, *Butch Cassidy and the Sundance Kid*, *Airport* and *Love Story* had a strong influence on American cinema. In addition, the majority of the Top 14 also had enormous prestige and were celebrated, both by the film industry itself and by the press, as major artistic achievements, while also being identified as all-time audience favourites in several polls. The immediate impact made by *The Graduate* is particularly striking. It was on the annual 'Ten Best' list (including both American and foreign films) of the *New York Times* (Steinberg 1980: 174); won Best Direction at the New York Film Critics Awards for 1967 (1980: 269); was named as one of the ten 'Best English-Language Films' of the year by the National Board of Review (1980: 281); won Golden Globes from the Hollywood Foreign Press Association for Best Musical/Comedy as well as Best Director, Best Actress and Most Promising Newcomer (both male and female) (1980: 294); was chosen as the Best-Written American Comedy by the Writers Guild of America (1980: 314), given the award for Best Director by the Directors Guild of America (1980: 320) and nominated for seven Academy Awards, winning the one for Best Director (Elley 2000: 337). What is even more remarkable is that, within a few years, *The Graduate* was considered one of the all-time greats. In 1970, it was selected as one of the ten best films (both American and foreign) of the 1960s by *Time* magazine (Steinberg 1980: 178); and in two *Los Angeles Times* surveys conducted that year, both the newspaper's readers and a group of filmmakers voted *The Graduate* the best film of the 1960s (again both American and foreign films were being considered) (1980: 145). When the University of Southern California asked a panel of American filmmakers and critics in 1972 to name 'the most significant movies in American cinema history', that is 'films which gave new concepts and advanced the art and technique of filmmaking', *The Graduate* made it into the top thirty (1980: 186–7). Finally, in a 1977 *Los Angeles Times* readers' poll about the best American films of all time, *The Graduate* came in at no. 14 (1980: 189).

The Graduate was by no means alone among the Top 14 in receiving such recognition. The 1977 *Los Angeles Times* list also featured *One Flew Over the Cuckoo's Nest*, *The Godfather* and *Rocky* in the top twenty. When the American Film Institute (AFI) conducted what was probably the largest survey of its kind in 1977, asking its 35,000 members for the greatest American films ever, the top fifty included *The Sting*, *Rocky*, *One Flew Over the Cuckoo's Nest*, *Jaws*, *The Graduate*, *The Godfather* and *Butch Cassidy and the Sundance Kid* (Steinberg 1980: 144). In addition to *The Graduate*, *The Godfather* and *American Graffiti* made it onto the annual 'Ten Best' lists of the *New York Times* and *Time*, while *Love Story*, *The Godfather*, *The Sting* and *Rocky* all made it onto the National Board of Review's annual lists of the ten best English-language films, with *The Sting* getting the award for best English-language film of the year. *Butch Cassidy and the Sundance Kid*, *The Godfather*, *Blazing Saddles* and *One Flew Over the Cuckoo's Nest* all won screenplay awards from the Writers Guild of America, and the Directors Guild gave its director awards to *The Godfather*, *The Sting*, *One Flew Over the Cuckoo's Nest* and *Rocky*. *Love Story*, *The Godfather*,

The Exorcist, *One Flew Over the Cuckoo's Nest* and *Rocky* all won multiple Golden Globes, including those for Best Drama, while *American Graffiti* won for Best Musical/Comedy.

Finally, between them, the Top 14 won numerous Oscars, in several years completely dominating the awards ceremony (see entries on individual films in Elley 2000). In 1969 *Butch Cassidy and the Sundance Kid* won four Oscars (including Best Screenplay) from seven nominations (including Best Picture and Director). The following year, *Love Story* won one award (Best Score) from seven nominations (including all five major categories: Best Picture, Director, Actor, Actress and Screenplay), while *Airport* had one win (Best Supporting Actress) from ten nominations (including Best Picture). Nominations in the Best Picture and Director categories indicate that the film in question was considered as a major artistic achievement by people working in the film industry, even if it did not win. However, it is, of course, the winning of these awards which most clearly signals to the world what Hollywood regards as its greatest films. In 1972, *The Godfather* won Best Picture, Actor and Screenplay from eleven nominations. *The Sting* ruled the 1973 ceremony, with seven wins (including Best Picture, Director and Screenplay) from ten nominations; only seven films in Hollywood history had ever received more Oscars (Steinberg 1980: 258). *American Graffiti* won nothing, but was nominated five times (including Best Picture, Director and Screenplay), while *The Exorcist* won Best Screenplay and Sound from ten nominations (including Best Picture and Director). In 1974, *The Towering Inferno* won three awards (Best Cinematography, Song and Editing) from eight nominations, which included Best Picture. *One Flew Over the Cuckoo's Nest* swept the 1975 Academy Awards; nominated for ten Oscars, it won in all the five major categories, which had only happened once before in Academy history (*It Happened One Night*, 1934). While *Jaws* was nominated for Best Picture, it only won Best Sound, Score and Editing. Finally, with awards for Best Picture, Director and Editing (from ten nominations) *Rocky* was the main winner in 1976.

Again and again during the decade from 1967 to 1976 did the film industry publicly declare its biggest commercial hits to be amongst its greatest films, and in four out of ten years, the undisputed overall winners at the Academy Awards belonged to the Top 14. There is a remarkable consistency in the Academy Award performance of this group of films. Indeed, even the two films which were not recognised by the Academy with a Best

Picture or Best Director nomination, were nominated in other categories: *Blazing Saddles* received three nominations (without a win), while *The Poseidon Adventure* had one win from eight nominations. When also considering the other awards mentioned above as well as the 'Ten Best' lists, readers' surveys and critics' polls from the late 1960s to the late 1970s, the amount of recognition the Top 14 received – as the best and/or the most significant and/or as favourites – is impressive indeed. This is yet another confirmation for the absolute centrality of the Top 14 in the film culture of their time.

Having established their centrality, we can now ask whether the New Hollywood Top 14 are a distinctive set of films. In other words, do these fourteen films have a lot in common with each other, and are they clearly distinguished from the big hits of earlier and later periods? The comparison with the biggest hits of the years since 1977 will have to wait until the conclusion. So what about the biggest hits before 1967?

The Roadshow Era Top 14, 1949–66

Thomas Schatz (1993), Sheldon Hall (2002) and Steve Neale (2003) have all offered succinct surveys of the biggest hits across American film history, concentrating on those films which were both unusally expensive and exceptionally successful at the box office. Since the 1950s, these films have commonly been known as 'blockbusters'; indeed, during this decade Hollywood was gripped by a 'blockbuster mentality' (Hall 2002: 11; Neale 2003: 47; Schatz 1993: 12). From the 1910s to the 1940s, the American film industry very occasionally produced a film that left the competition far behind. Even when their numerous re-releases are discounted, both D. W. Griffith's Civil War epic *The Birth of a Nation* (1915) and Walt Disney's animated feature *Snow White and the Seven Dwarfs* (1937) earned twice as much as their closest competitors in the decades before 1939 (Finler 2003: 356–7). Then, in 1939/40, David O. Selznick's Civil War epic *Gone With the Wind*, during the first of its many releases, multiplied the previous record. While this new record was not broken in the 1940s, the number of extremely high-grossing films increased dramatically. Comparisons across decades are notoriously difficult because of ticket price inflation, yet it is safe to say that the level of commercial success achieved so uniquely by *Snow White and the Seven Dwarfs* ($8m rentals) in the 1930s, became a still rare, but quite regular occurrence during the 1940s. Then, it pretty much became an annual event, beginning with Cecil B. DeMille's biblical epic *Samson and Delilah* in 1949.

There are further reasons for identifying 1949 as the starting point of a new era in American film history. To begin with, during the previous year, the unfavourable Supreme Court ruling in the so-called Paramount case, in which the major Hollywood studios had been accused of monopolistic practices, marked the definite end of an era. Most importantly, the ruling outlawed vertical integration, that is the combination of film production, distribution and exhibition within the same company, which had been the cornerstone of the Hollywood studio system since the 1920s. Without their American theatre chains (which gradually gained their independence in the late 1940s and early 1950s), the Hollywood majors had to find new ways of doing business. At the same time, they felt the effects of a spectacular decline in cinema attendance which had started in 1947. The average weekly attendance – which had been relatively stable for several years at record heights – plummeted from 82m in 1946 to 73m in 1947; thereafter the annual loss of about 10 per cent of the audience continued until in 1952 average weekly attendance was only 42m, that is about half the 1946 figure (Finler 2003: 378). After a temporary, slight recovery in the mid-1950s, attendance levels dropped further until, from 1966 onwards, they stabilised (with only minor fluctuations for the next two decades) at less than a quarter of the 1946 attendance (2003: 379). Throughout this period, foreign markets became ever more important, especially continental Europe, where cinema audiences were in fact growing across most of the 1950s (Hall 1999: vol. 1, 325–7; Krämer 2000: 197–8).

Television was not responsible for the initial audience decline in the US (because few people owned a set in the late 1940s when this decline set in), but it certainly was a major reason for the ongoing reduction in ticket sales. Television ownership increased from 9 per cent of all US households in 1950 to 93 per cent in 1966 (Finler 2003: 375). 1954 was the first year in which more than half of all households had TV, offering daily entertainment which included numerous, yet mostly minor films that had originally been made for, and shown in, movie theatres (see Lafferty 1990: 236–40). From 1955 onwards the number of theatrical movies on TV exploded, now including a wealth of important pre-1948 releases from the major studios (1990: 240–2). In 1961 movies, which had previously been shown mainly on independent local TV stations, became a staple of network programming; NBC's *Saturday Night at the Movies* included films made after 1948 and became a prime-time success, especially with young, urban viewers (1990: 245).

The Supreme Court ruling, the drop in attendance levels and the increasing availability of movies on television created a situation in which the major Hollywood studios began to make fewer, more expensive films and came to depend heavily on the blockbuster success of their main releases. Initially, in the late 1940s and early 1950s, in the wake of the much reduced production levels of the war years, the major studios increased their output, but after 1953 – partly because more old movies were becoming accessible to more people on television – the studios' feature film output declined once again, never to recover (Finler 2003: 364). An industry which had previously revolved around mass production and habitual consumption (with one- to two-thirds of the population going to the cinema every week) now became hit driven, with major blockbuster success depending on a film's ability to draw in the large majority of the American population who had stopped going to the cinema on a weekly basis (see Jowett 1976: 478). Such success also depended increasingly on a film's ability to attract foreign audiences, especially in Europe, where cinemagoers tended to prefer European-themed Hollywood imports (often based on European source material, shot on European locations and featuring European stars) to more specifically American films (Garncarz 1994: 103–5; Krämer 2002a: 231–2).

As noted above, almost every year from 1949 onwards saw the release of one or more films which left the competition in the US (and also often in foreign markets) far behind (see appendix 3). The breakaway success of *Samson and Delilah* in 1949 (with $12m rentals) was followed by that of another Biblical epic, *Quo Vadis* ($12m), in 1951. One year later, another Cecil B. DeMille spectacular, the circus drama *The Greatest Show on Earth* earned $14m. Like *The Birth of a Nation*, *Snow White and the Seven Dwarfs* and *Gone With the Wind*, these three films were roadshows, that is, they were first presented in only a few showcase theatres, where they had very long runs (often for years) at premium prices, usually with separate performances (unlike the usual practice of running films continuously across the day), advance bookings, orchestral overtures and intermissions. After a while, mostly while the original roadshow run was still going on, these films also received a general release at regular prices in regular cinemas. In various published and unpublished manuscripts, Sheldon

Hall has explored the roadshow phenomenon across American film history (see, for example, Hall 1999 and 2002). He has noted that after the Second World War Hollywood invested more heavily than ever before in an increasing number of films intended for roadshow release, and that almost all of the big hits from 1949 to 1966 were roadshows. This period, then, can best be understood as the 'Roadshow Era'. The Roadshow Era came into its own with the introduction of various spectacular widescreen formats in 1952/53. *This is Cinerama* (1952), a travelogue introducing the most spectacular format (making use of three projectors and a massive curved screen), earned $15m, and the biblical epic *The Robe* (1953), the first CinemaScope release, earned $18m. In subsequent years, both the number of movies earning $12m and more, and the earnings of the true breakaway hits increased, culminating with *The Sound of Music* (1965) which generated $80m.

Due to ticket price inflation, figures across the Roadshow Era are not comparable. Average ticket prices rose from 38c in 1949 to $1.09 in 1966 and premium ticket prices for roadshow presentations also rose (Finler 2003: 378–9). If this inflation is taken into account, the Top 14 for this period are as follows (see appendix 4):

1952   *The Greatest Show on Earth* (with non-adjusted rentals of $14m)
1953   *The Robe* ($18m)
1956   *The Ten Commandments* ($43m) and *Around the World in Eighty Days* ($23m)
1957   *The Bridge on the River Kwai* ($17m)
1959   *Ben-Hur* ($37m)
1961   *West Side Story* ($20m)
1963   *Cleopatra* ($26m)
1964   *My Fair Lady* ($34m), *Mary Poppins* ($31m) and *Goldfinger* ($23m)
1965   *The Sound of Music* ($80m), *Doctor Zhivago* ($47m) and *Thunderball* ($29m)

With the exception of *Mary Poppins* and the two James Bond films, *Goldfinger* and *Thunderball*, these were all roadshows. For the purposes of calculating their market shares, I will assume that these films, which often ran for years, earned all rentals in their year of release (indeed, most films earned a fair share of their overall rentals during the early stages of their release). To determine approximate figures for box office grosses, I simply double the rental figures. *The Greatest Show on Earth* has the smallest market share. Its $28m gross makes up just over 2 per cent of total revenues from ticket sales in 1952 ($1,246m), while all the other films have market shares over 3 per cent (Finler 2003: 376–7). The $160m gross of *The Sound of Music* constitutes a staggering 17 per cent of the total revenues in 1965 ($927m). If we look across the fourteen years from 1952 to 1965, the total box office gross of the fourteen top hits (one per year) was $884m; this is 6 per cent of the total box office revenues during these years ($14,976m). This percentage is lower, but comparable to the one for 1967–76. Counting only the top ten films for the decade (again one per year), their total gross of $1,402m amounts to 10 per cent of the total income from ticket sales ($14,656).

It is difficult to determine how many tickets each of the roadshows sold, because prices during the initial roadshow release were well above the average ticket price, which only applied to the tickets sold when the film later went on general release. Let us therefore assume that, across the roadshow and regular releases, the ticket prices for these films were 50 per cent higher than the average ticket price in their year of release. Hence, we can estimate that *The Greatest Show on Earth*, with a $28m gross, sold 41m tickets for an average 69c (50 per cent more than the average ticket price of 46c in 1952) (Finler 2003: 378). This was the equivalent of 26 per cent of the American population in 1952 (157m) (Wattenberg 1976: 8). According to the same calculation, *The Sound of Music* sold 106m tickets during its first release, the equivalent of 55 per cent of the 1965 population (194m). Because *Thunderball* was not a roadshow, we can use the average ticket price for 1965 ($1.01), which means that the film sold almost 58m tickets, the equivalent of 30 per cent of the American population. While some of the above figures are only rough estimates, they do indicate that population percentages for Roadshow Era superhits are comparable to those calculated for the New Hollywood Top 14.

The tie-ins with best-selling soundtracks are also extensive. The following Roadshow Era Top 14 soundtracks were listed in *Billboard*'s annual top ten (which started in 1957): *Around the World in Eighty Days* (no. 4 in 1957 and no. 6 in 1958); *West Side Story* (no. 1/1962, no. 1/1963, no. 4/1964); *Mary Poppins* (no. 1/1965); *My Fair Lady* (no. 4/1965); *The Sound of Music* (no. 3/1965, no. 2/1966, no. 3/1967); *Doctor Zhivago* (no. 7/1966 and no. 3/1967) (*People* 2000: 223). Unlike the New Hollywood Top 14, many of the Roadshow Era superhits were adaptations of Broadway musicals, two of which – *My Fair Lady* (running from 1956 to 1962) and *The Sound of Music* (1959–63) – had been among the fifteen longest-running shows in Broadway history up to that point (*People* 2000: 327). What is perhaps even more important is the success of the original cast albums for the Broadway shows: *My Fair Lady* was no. 1 in 1957 and 1958 as well as no. 9 in 1959; *The Sound of Music* was no. 1 in 1960, no. 4 in 1961 and no. 5 in 1962; the original cast album of *West Side Story* joined the film soundtrack in the top ten of 1962 (at no. 2) (*People* 2000: 223). Between them, original cast and soundtrack albums for the Top 14 of the Roadshow Era dominated album charts from 1957 to 1966, with a strong presence even in 1967.

The connection between the Top 14 and best-selling books was equally extensive. To begin with, three of the films told stories related to the biggest best-seller of all time, the Bible. Indeed, the Revised Standard Version of the Bible was the best-selling non-fiction hardcover of 1953 (the year *The Robe* was released) and 1954 (*People* 2000: 299). Also in 1953, Lloyd C. Douglas' novel *The Robe* was at the top of the fiction chart; the book had been in the top ten every year between 1942 and 1945, mostly in one of the two top spots, before the release of the film adaptation revived its sales. Only a few years before the release of *The Ten Commandments*, books about Moses had been in the fiction and the non-fiction top ten. While Lew Wallace's *Ben-Hur* (first published in 1880) did not re-appear in the charts in the 1950s, it had been one of the best-selling books in American publishing history up to that point (Mott 1947: 173–4, 261). *Doctor Zhivago*, which had won the Nobel Prize for Boris Pasternak in 1958, had also been the best-selling fiction hardcover in that year, slipping to no. 2 in 1959. *Around the World in Eighty Days* and *Mary Poppins* were based on classic stories (by Jules Verne and P. L. Travers, respectively) and *The Bridge on the River Kwai* on a recent book by Pierre Boulle. The two James Bond films were based on novels by best-selling author Ian Fleming, whose *You Only Live Twice* was the eighth best-selling novel of 1964, while *The Man With the Golden Gun* was at no. 7 in 1965. Over the years, most of Fleming's books and also some of the other novels adapted into breakaway blockbuster movies during the Roadshow Era sold millions of copies; these books included *Thunderball* (4.2m copies sold by 1975) and *Goldfinger* (3.7m) as

FIGURE 3 *The Sound of Music* (Robert Wise, 1965)

well as *Doctor Zhivago* (5m), *The Robe* (3.7m) and *The Bridge on the River Kwai* (2m) (Hackett & Burke 1977: 11–19).

As the theatrical adaptations did with the Broadway shows and original cast albums, the literary adaptations drew on the often massive popularity of their source material, but they also, most likely, helped to sell millions of paperbacks. In any case, just like the New Hollywood Top 14, the Top 14 of the Roadshow Era resonated widely and deeply across American culture in the 1950s and 1960s. They also had a tremendous impact on subsequent film production and the success of future releases. The cycle of hugely successful Biblical epics, from *Samson and Delilah* to *Ben-Hur*, inspired filmmakers and studio executives to give a range of historical topics an epic treatment. This resulted in several cycles of historical epics, that is, films which set their stories of personal struggle and love against the spectacular backdrop of key moments in (mostly Western) history. These cycles included ancient epics like *Spartacus* (the highest-grossing film of 1960) and *Cleopatra* (1st/1963); medieval epics such as *El Cid* (3rd/1961); nineteenth-century epics like *How the West Was Won* (1st/1962) and *Hawaii* (1st/1966); and twentieth-century epics including *Giant* (3rd/1956), *Doctor Zhivago* (2nd/1965) and *The Sand Pebbles* (4th/1966) as well as epic Second World War films such as *From Here to Eternity* (2nd/1953), *The Bridge on the River Kwai* (1st/1957), *The Guns of Navarone* (2nd/1961) and *The Longest Day* (2nd/1962).

Historical epics in turn gave a boost to prestigious historical dramas – notably *Tom Jones* (3rd/1963) and *A Man For All Seasons* (5th/1966) – and to spectacular historical adventures, that is, films focusing on (often comic) action rather than the processes of historical change. These included *20,000 Leagues Under the Sea* (3rd/1954) and *Around the World in Eighty Days* (2nd/1956) as well as *Those Magnificent Men in Their Flying Machines* (4th/1965) and *The Great Race* (5th/1965). The string of superhit musicals from *West Side Story* to *The Sound of Music* – which, in turn, had built on the success of earlier musicals from *Jolson Sings Again* (3rd/1949) to *South Pacific* (1st/1958) – also had a major impact on American film culture, which would be felt in the overproduction of big-budget musicals after 1966.

Thus, the Roadshow Era Top 14 helped to shape film production and hit patterns across the 1950s and 1960s. Finally, like the New Hollywood Top 14, they received widespread recognition from critics, from the Academy and in audience polls. Ten of the fourteen were included on the annual 'Ten Best' lists of the *New York Times*, three made it onto the *Time* lists between 1952 and 1961 (the list was not compiled from 1962 to 1966), and seven were ranked among the annual top ten of the National Board of Review (Steinberg 1980: 172–4, 176–8, 278–81).

Five of the fourteen were recognised as the Best Picture of the year by the Los Angeles Film Critics Association, and nine won Golden Globes for Best Drama or Best Musical/Comedy from the Hollywood Foreign Press Association (1980: 267–9, 288–93). When a representative sample of cinemagoers were asked about the best film they had seen in 1965, the resulting chart was headed by *The Sound of Music*, followed by *Mary Poppins*, *Goldfinger*, *Cleopatra* and *My Fair Lady*, Top 14 films which had been released in preceding years, but had extended runs across the decade (Anon. 1965a). A later survey of women found that their favourite films during 1966 were *The Sound of Music*, *Doctor Zhivago* and *My Fair Lady* (Anon. 1967a). In a readers' survey conducted by the *Los Angeles Times* in 1967, both *Ben-Hur* and *Around the World in Eighty Days* made it onto the list of their twenty all-time favourites (Steinberg 1980: 189).

In addition to their overwhelming recognition by both critics and audiences, the Roadshow Era Top 14 also dominated award ceremonies organised by the film industry itself. Four won screenplay awards from the Writers Guild of America and five won the director award from the Directors Guild (Steinberg 1980: 312–13, 318–19). Except for the two James Bond films, all of the Top 14 were nominated for Best Picture (as well as numerous other Oscars), and seven won this award (as well as numerous others) (see entries for each film in Elley 2000). In 1957, *The Bridge on the River Kwai* won a total of seven Oscars, including an almost clean sweep of the five major categories (not surprisingly, Best Actress was missing). In 1959 *Ben-Hur* won a record eleven Oscars, which was almost matched by the ten Oscars for *West Side Story* in 1961. *My Fair Lady* dominated the 1964 ceremony with eight wins and *Mary Poppins* won five that year, while, between them, *The Sound of Music* and *Doctor Zhivago* won ten Oscars in 1965.

Just like the New Hollywood Top 14 from 1967 to 1976, the Top 14 of the Roadshow Era dominated American film culture in every conceivable way between 1949 and 1966. While their level of dominance is the same, the two sets of films are very different.

The Top 14s in comparison

The distinctive characteristics of the New Hollywood Top 14 can best be observed after first establishing commonalities among the Roadshow Era Top 14. With the exception of *The Greatest Show on Earth*, the films can easily be grouped into three broad categories: historical epics – both biblical (*The Robe*, *The Ten Commandments*, *Ben-Hur*) and non-Biblical (*The Bridge on the River Kwai*, *Cleopatra*, *Doctor Zhivago*), musicals – with both historical (*Mary Poppins*, *The Sound of Music*) and contemporary (*West Side Story*) settings, and international adventures – again both historical (*Around the World in Eighty Days*) and contemporary (*Goldfinger* and *Thunderball*). What is more, the three categories are closely connected insofar as *The Sound of Music* has an epic dimension, setting its central story against the rise of fascism. All of the epics and two of the three musicals have non-American settings, and apart from *The Bridge on the River Kwai* none of these films feature any American characters, while their non-American protagonists are almost all played by foreigners, mostly British actors. This internationalism is shared by the international adventures, which take place mostly outside the US and feature only a few American supporting characters, with the non-American main characters again being played by British actors. (As suggested above, this internationalism helped many of these films to succeed in foreign markets.)

Another important feature of the Roadshow Era Top 14 is that, with the exception of *Mary Poppins*, *Thunderball* and *Goldfinger*, they were all roadshows. A roadshow release signalled the special status of the film, setting it apart from the kinds of films that people might attend habitually. Attendance at a roadshow had all the trappings of a rare, expensive and prestigious outing to a legitimate theatre, and even when the film went on general release some of this prestige and event status was likely to remain attached to it. The extraordinary length of these films (mostly between two and a half and four hours at a time when 90–100 minutes was still the norm), and their widely publicised, huge budgets confirmed that their makers had gone out of their way to offer audiences an overwhelming, in many ways unique experience (this also applies to *Mary Poppins*). An average release by one of the major studios cost about $1m to make in 1949 and $1.5m in the early 1960s (Steinberg 1980: 50), yet even a comparatively cheap roadshow like *The Bridge on the River Kwai* had a budget of $2.9m in 1957, while *The Ten Commandments* ($13m) and *Cleopatra* ($40m) broke all existing records (for budgets of these and other Top 14 films, see Finler 2003: 95, 123, 154, 190, 244, 269, 298, 331).

Given their budgets and roadshow presentation, the Roadshow Era superhits, except for the two Bond films, clearly were calculated blockbuster hits, that is, they were geared towards the largest possible audience and needed to reach it to make a profit (this is not to say that all such films are successful, as will be discussed in the next chapter). Despite potentially controversial elements (most notably eroticism and brutality) in some of the films, the roadshows and *Mary Poppins* were basically addressed to an all-inclusive family audience. With the exception of *The Bridge on the River Kwai*, these films also highlight elements which have traditionally been associated more with female than with male audiences: romance, familial love, sentimentality, lavish costumes and/or song and dance (more about this in the next chapter). Interestingly, several of these films gave first billing to their female leads and were clearly built around their performances: Betty Hutton in *The Greatest Show on Earth*, Natalie Wood in *West Side Story*, Elizabeth Taylor in *Cleopatra*, Julie Andrews in *Mary Poppins* and *The Sound of Music*, and Audrey Hepburn in *My Fair Lady*.

In many ways, the two Bond films stand apart from the other twelve films in the Roadshow Era Top 14. They were not given roadshow releases, had lower (albeit still above average) budgets and foregrounded elements such as sex and violence that have traditionally been associated with male audiences, especially male youth, while at the same time being regarded as inappropriate for children. Whether children were actually kept away from Bond films in the mid-1960s and to what extent women disliked them is difficult to determine. Nevertheless, the two Bond superhits provide a transition to the blockbuster successes of the New Hollywood.

With the exception of *Airport*, none of the New Hollywood Top 14 had a full-blown traditional roadshow presentation. Nevertheless, some of the Top 14 were given special releases, starting out in a small number of theatres, sometimes in a special format (70mm) and occasionally demanding premium ticket prices, before being released more widely. According to Sheldon Hall this applied, to a greater or lesser extent, to *The Godfather*, *The Poseidon Adventure*, *The Exorcist* and *The Towering Inferno*. These films had above-average budgets and length, but they did not match the extremes of the Roadshow Era Top 14, not even *The Towering Inferno*, which ran for 165 minutes and cost $15m to make at a time when the average budget for a release from a major studio was $2.5m (Steinberg 1980: 50). The other nine films varied in length between less than 100 minutes (*Love Story*, 99 mins; *Blazing Saddles*, 93min) and just over two hours (*The Sting*, 127 mins; *One Flew Over the Cuckoo's Nest*, 133 mins), and also in cost, with *American Graffiti* ($0.7m) and *Rocky* ($1.5m) at the lower end – well below the average budget – and *Jaws* ($12m) at the top end (Finler 2003: 95, 123, 154, 190, 244, 269, 298, 331). The big-budget special releases, the vehicles for top stars (such as Paul Newman and Robert Redford in both *Butch Cassidy and the Sundance Kid* and *The Sting* and Jack Nicholson in *One Flew Over the Cuckoo's Nest*) and the films based on huge best-

FIGURE 4 *The Godfather* (Francis Ford Coppola, 1971)

sellers could reasonably have been expected to do well at the box office – they were calculated blockbusters – but *The Graduate, American Graffiti, Blazing Saddles* and *Rocky* were big surprises.

The presence of several surprise hits, then, is one of the distinctive features of the New Hollywood Top 14, prefigured, one might say, by the transitional Bond films – although these were sequels and therefore no longer a true surprise; the level of their success was, however, unexpected. Another distinctive feature is the absence of epics, musicals and international adventures from the New Hollywood Top 14. True, *The Godfather* is a historical drama with epic scope, but it does not deal directly with important developments in Western history, although it may be understood as an allegory thereof. While the roadshow epics depicted transformative events affecting whole societies and the course of subsequent history (the liberation of the Israelites and the delivery of the ten commandments, the fall of the Egyptian empire, the crucifixion of Christ and the beginnings of Christianity, the Russian Revolution and the Second World War), *The Godfather* portrays the development of a criminal organisation in the form of a family drama.

Of the four other films in the Top 14 with historical settings, *Butch Cassidy and the Sundance Kid* and *Blazing Saddles* deal with the disappearance of the Old West, yet they hardly do so with the seriousness and the excessive spectacular displays so characteristic of the epic (see Sobchak 1990). Set in 1962, *American Graffiti* also deals with the end of an era (the 'fifties'), but this is only made explicit at the very end, when the on-screen text outlines the subsequent fate of the four male leads (one missing in action in Vietnam, another living in Canada, presumably to evade the draft). *The Sting*, finally, is tightly focused on friendships and enmities in the criminal world of 1930s America.

As to international adventures, it is noticeable that with the exception of *The Poseidon Adventure*, which is set on an oceanliner in international waters, the Top 14 are all set in the United States, with only a few scenes in *Butch Cassidy and the Sundance Kid*, *The Godfather* and *The Exorcist* venturing abroad. Finally, one might say that the musical tradition is still resonating in the New Hollywood Top 14, what with the importance of pop songs on the soundtracks especially of *The Graduate* and *American Graffiti*, but apart from a few scenes in *Blazing Saddles* and perhaps *The Godfather*, characters do not express themselves through song and dance.

If the New Hollywood Top 14, unlike the superhits of the Roadshow Era, are neither epics nor international adventures nor musicals, what are they? By and large, it is much more difficult to group them together. Most clearly related are the three disaster films. One might put *The Graduate* and *Love Story* together as romantic comedy-dramas (with the former mainly comedic, the latter mainly dramatic). *Butch Cassidy and the Sundance Kid*, *The Sting* and *Blazing Saddles* are buddy movies focusing on male friendship; one could stretch this category to include three other films centring on male partnerships or friendships (*The Godfather*, *Jaws* and *One Flew Over the Cuckoo's Nest*). Or one might group together historical comedy-dramas (*Butch Cassidy and the Sundance Kid*, *The Sting*, *American Graffiti* and *Blazing Saddles*) and the closely related historical drama *The Godfather*. Alternatively, one might use more established genre categories, describing *The Godfather* as a gangster film and *The Sting* perhaps as a gangster comedy; *Butch Cassidy and the Sundance Kid* and *Blazing Saddles* as westerns; *The Exorcist* as a horror film and also perhaps *Jaws*. *One Flew Over the Cuckoo's Nest* and *Rocky* might both be described as contemporary dramas.

Obviously, the possibility to apply a multiplicity of labels to individual films is in the nature of popular cinema and not unique to the New Hollywood Top 14. Steve Neale has shown that the marketing and reception of any particular Hollywood film usually involves a range of generic terms rather than tying the film down to a single genre (2000: Ch. 7). However, the above discussion suggests that, in terms of generic labelling, the New Hollywood superhits are a much more diverse set than the Roadshow Era Top 14 (to follow up this suggestion it would be necessary to examine the generic terms used, for example, on posters and in reviews for these films). At the same time, it has to be noted that, while being generically diverse, the New Hollywood superhits are more restricted in terms of temporal and spatial settings than the ones from the Roadshow Era. The stories take place – primarily and in most cases exclusively – in the US during the nineteenth and twentieth centuries, mostly in the 1960s and 1970s. By contrast, the settings of the Roadshow Era Top 14 range around the globe (quite literally in *Around the World in Eighty Days*), with Egypt and Palestine, Rome and London, Russia and Austria featured prominently. The timeframe ranges from more than one thousand years BC to the 1960s. Only four films are set in contemporary times, only two primarily in the US, whereas the

New Hollywood Top 14 are all, as we have seen, primarily set in the US, and only five are set in the past.

Another notable difference between the two sets of films is the dramatically increased prominence of potentially controversial elements in New Hollywood superhits. Compared to the very strict, traditional, often explicitly religious morality of most of the Roadshow Era Top 14 (with the exception of the Bond films and, possibly, *The Bridge on the River Kwai*), the largely sympathetic portrayals of criminals in *Butch Cassidy and the Sundance Kid*, *The Godfather*, *The Sting* and *One Flew Over the Cuckoo's Nest* seem daring, as do the casual affairs (adulterous and otherwise) or one-off sexual encounters and occasional (near) nudity in several of the films (notably *The Graduate*, *Butch Cassidy and the Sundance Kid*, *American Graffiti* and *One Flew Over the Cuckoo's Nest*). Similarly transgressive are the (comical) racial slurs and scenes of interracial sex in *Blazing Saddles*. Then there are scenes of intense and graphic violence in *The Godfather* (where the climactic massacre is presented explicitly as sacrilegious), *The Exorcist* (where the most shocking violence is sexualised as well as sacrilegious), *Jaws* (with its protracted killing at the beginning, its dismembered bodies and its climactic death of one of the protagonists who is half swallowed by a shark), *One Flew Over the Cuckoo's Nest* (with its electric shock therapy, bloody suicide and climactic mercy killing) and *Rocky* (with its graphic boxing scenes). In the final scene of *Butch Cassidy and the Sundance Kid* the violent death of the two protagonists in a hail of bullets is evoked through the sound of countless shots being fired, while the image is frozen on the precise moment before their bodies are hit.

Several of these films were widely perceived as being unsuitable for children. The clearest indication of this is their ratings. *The Godfather*, *The Exorcist* and *One Flew Over the Cuckoo's Nest* all received an 'R', which meant that those under 17 could not attend without an adult. Only one of the New Hollywood Top 14 (*Airport*) received a 'G' (suitable for general audiences). *The Graduate* was released before the ratings system was introduced in 1968, but upon re-release it received a 'PG' (parental guidance suggested) like most of the others. When the Roadshow Era Top 14 received belated ratings, most of them, by contrast, had a 'G', that is, their status as family entertainment was confirmed. The others received 'GP' ratings, which were later retitled 'PG' (more about the meaning of these in chapter two). These films were *Thunderball* (rated in 1970), *Goldfinger* (1971) and

Doctor Zhivago (1971); *The Bridge on the River Kwai* received a 'PG' rating in 1991 (see the MPAA website, http://www.mpaa.org/movieratings).

It is also reasonable to assume that many of the New Hollywood Top 14 appealed to males more than to females. The stories of all Top 14 films revolve around the experiences, desires and actions of men. Male bonding, sometimes combined with intense male rivalry and conflict, is central to many of the films. Close male relationships are at the centre of *The Sting*, *Butch Cassidy and the Sundance Kid*, *The Godfather*, *American Graffiti*, *Blazing Saddles*, *Jaws* and *One Flew Over the Cuckoo's Nest*; to a lesser extent this also applies to *The Exorcist* and *The Towering Inferno*. In many cases, women are marginalised to the point where they disappear altogether, as in the final part of *Jaws*, in long stretches of *The Godfather* and *The Sting* as well as much of *Butch Cassidy and the Sundance Kid*. In *The Exorcist* the focus shifts dramatically from a mother and her daughter to a battle between a male-identified demon and two priests. *American Graffiti* deals with romantic relationships as well as with male friendships, but the women are dropped from the final titles outlining the future lives of the protagonists. In only three of the films does a woman receive top billing (Anne Bancroft in *The Graduate*, Ali McGraw in *Love Story* and Ellen Burstyn in *The Exorcist*). Romantic love is central only to a few of the films, notably *The Graduate* and *Love Story*, but even these two films – like all of the Top 14 – focus primarily on male protagonists. Where male/female relationships are foregrounded, they are characterised by seemingly unresolvable problems. At the end of *The Graduate*, the re-united couple is facing an uncertain future with somewhat blank or puzzled looks on their faces. At the end of *Love Story*, the protagonist's wife is dead. In *One Flew Over the Cuckoo's Nest* the institution the hero rebels against is personified by a woman, who destroys him in the end. At the conclusion of *Rocky*, the proud, but defeated protagonist cries out for the woman he loves, but this privileging of romance takes place in the hyper-masculine setting of the boxing arena. On all levels, then, women are sidelined (or vilified) on screen and also therefore, one may assume, in the audience (although there is no doubt the sex appeal of male stars such as Paul Newman and Robert Redford and also the possibility that women make an emotional investment in male/male relationships; see Jenkins 1992: ch. 6).

Possibly connected to this gender bias is the emphasis of several of the New Hollywood Top 14 on organisational structures and professional activities. *Airport* explores the complex operations of an airport and the particular skills needed by managers, pilots and technicians. *The Towering Inferno* examines irresponsible building practices employed by large corporations and features firefighters as well as architects. *Jaws* focuses on a policeman, a scientist and a fisherman and includes a lot of details on the responsibilities and limitations of police work, the biology and behaviour of sharks as well as the mechanics of shark hunting. *One Flew Over the Cuckoo's Nest* examines the operations of a mental institution, prominently featuring nurses and their varied day-to-day activities. *The Exorcist* presents, in often excruciating detail, both the failure of medicine to treat the young protagonist, and then the success of the exorcism systematically executed by two priests (who are authorised by the Catholic Church). *The Godfather* is almost wholly concerned with the portrayal of a complex criminal organisation, its hierarchies and strategies, its internal and external rivalries. *Rocky* offers insights into the boxing world, depicting training regimes and fights as well as behind-the-scenes machinations. An interesting variation on this procedural emphasis is offered by *The Sting*, in which con-artists set up an intricate organisation so as to take revenge for one of their own. While such procedural elements were already present in the Roadshow Era Top 14, especially *The Greatest Show on Earth*, *The Bridge on the River Kwai* and the James Bond films, they came to dominate many of the New Hollywood Top 14.

Another important difference between the two sets of films is the shift (prefigured by *West Side Story*) from the presence of numerous nationalities in the Roadshow Era to a focus on American ethnicities and race relations in the New Hollywood. The Egyptians, Romans, Israelites, Russians, Austrians and Brits of the Roadshow Era Top 14 give way to hyphenated Americans. Most notably, Italian-American characters are at the centre of *Love Story*, *The Godfather* and *Rocky*, and there are the priest's immigrant mother and a Jewish policeman in *The Exorcist*, a Native American in *One Flew Over the Cuckoo's Nest*, and an old Jewish couple in *The Poseidon Adventure*. The protagonist of *Blazing Saddles* is black as are supporting characters in several of the other films, most notably the antagonist in *Rocky*. Finally, while not cast as Jewish characters in the Top 14, Dustin Hoffman, Gene Wilder (in *Blazing Saddles*) and Richard Dreyfuss (in both *American Graffiti* and *Jaws*) may have carried over a sense of Jewishness from other roles and from their off-screen publicity.

Finally, it is worth pointing out that through foregrounding both procedural elements and ethnicities, the New Hollywood Top 14 explore social divisions and group conflicts in American society, thus situating the localised personal conflicts they portray in a wider context. This is also achieved through an emphasis on class differences (for example between the lovers in *Love Story* and between the three protagonists of *Jaws*) and on generational differences (with, for example, young people rebelling against their parents in *The Graduate* and *Love Story* and, fantastically, in *The Exorcist*, while in *The Godfather* a young man first tries to leave the family business behind, but then takes over his father's role as the head of that business). While such social tensions are central to some of the Roadshow Era Top 14 (notably, around ethnicity in *West Side Story* and class in *My Fair Lady*), in the superhits of the earlier era conflicts within one society tend to be subordinated to international conflict or they are safely distanced by being located abroad and/or in the past (*West Side Story* being the exception, while the circus setting in *The Greatest Show on Earth* is presented as an international enclave within the US). By comparison, then, the New Hollywood Top 14 tell stories about deep divisions in American society, between institutions, professions, ethnicities, races, classes and generations. If the battle between the sexes is played down, it is because women are generally sidelined in these films.

Conclusion

American cinema of the years 1967–76, like that of the preceding era (1949–66), was dominated by a small group of films, which generated a significant portion of overall film industry income, were seen by up to half of the American population, had a mutually beneficial link to other best-selling cultural products (notably books and soundtracks), received widespread critical acclaim, were recognised by industry personnel as masterpieces and influenced future film production and hit patterns. As a group, the fourteen biggest hits of the New Hollywood contrasted in important ways with the fourteen superhits of the Roadshow Era. They included fewer special high-profile releases and more surprise hits than the earlier group of films, were generically more diversified but at the same time much more focused on contemporary American settings, dealt with American ethnicities rather than foreign nationalities and often explored organisations and professions as well as social divisions, in general were addressed more to men than to women and in some cases left the ideal of all-inclusive family entertainment far behind, mainly due to their prominent and graphic displays of sex and violence. The next chapter begins to explain how this dramatic shift came about.

2   FROM THE ROADSHOW ERA TO THE NEW HOLLYWOOD I

When *Time* magazine attempted to explain the Hollywood renaissance in 1967, it noted that, as the major studios' main goal continued to be 'to make money', a crucial factor in their changing output had to be that 'customers are now willing to pay for a different product' (Kanfer 1971: 324). This applied by no means to everyone; indeed, divisions within Hollywood's audience had become more pronounced than ever before: 'there is not a single cinema audience today but several'. While some people continued to prefer 'banality and bathos' in their cinematic entertainment, others wanted 'the intellectually demanding, emotionally fulfilling kind of film exemplified by *Bonnie and Clyde*' (ibid.). *Time* described generational differences as the most important fault line that Hollywood had to contend with, youth being on the side of innovation and older audiences on the side of tradition. The latter increasingly turned away from the cinema towards television which 'has all but taken over Hollywood's former function of providing placebo entertainment'. As a consequence, 'movie attendance among the middle-aged is down', while 'cinema has become the favorite art form of the young' (ibid.). An important factor in the rise of challenging youth-oriented films was the 'relaxation of censorship' (1971: 333). *Time* cautioned that 'the new thematic and technical freedom' constituted a threat to the integrity of filmmakers as well as an opportunity for innovation, because it might be 'used excessively for the sake of gimmickry or shock': 'Love scenes are not necessarily better because they are nuder' (1971: 324, 333). With respect to both sex and violence, the escalation of ever more graphic filmic representations was a distinct possibility.

Time's analysis concerned innovations across the Hollywood main-stream in the mid-1960s, but, of course, it could not yet address the changing patterns of success among Hollywood's superhits discussed in chapter one. Nevertheless, it is to be expected that the factors outlined by *Time* in 1967 contributed to the shift from the Roadshow Era Top 14 to the New Hollywood Top 14. In this chapter and the next, I extend the historical analysis offered by *Time* to explain the emergence of the New Hollywood Top 14 and related trends across the annual top ten from 1967 to 1976. My overarching question is the following: Why do certain kinds of films become extremely successful during a particular period, when during an earlier period the most successful films were of different kinds? The answer to this question first of all has to consider the types of films being produced, and the preferences expressed by audiences. Obviously, these two factors are closely connected, and their interplay is the focus of this chapter. As we will see, the film industry's output and audience preferences typically converge, but they can also be at odds with each other.

By and large the film industry aims to produce films that are liked by audiences, and it is therefore sensitive and responsive to changes in the audience. Such change may concern both the composition of the audience and the taste of particular groups. At the same time, audiences can only choose from what is on offer, and may well be dissatisfied with, even offended by, the industry's output. As a consequence, certain audience groups may go to the movies less frequently or stop going altogether. On the other hand, if new kinds of films are being released, audiences may develop new preferences and habits, or previously absent groups may now be attracted. In addition to being influenced by each other, industry output and audience preferences are in turn shaped by other factors, notably the re-organisation of the entertainment industry and changes in public opinion (to be discussed in chapter three).

The first section of this chapter examines the declining fortunes of traditional family-oriented roadshows, which had previously been so domi-nant but disappeared in the early 1970s. This is followed by a discussion of the production and success of taboo-breaking films. The final section concentrates on the rise of new kinds of family-oriented blockbusters (notably disaster movies) and the gradual return of the family audience in the mid-1970s.

The decline of family roadshows

The dominance of traditional roadshow epics and musicals was never more pronounced than in the early to mid-1960s, not only in the Top 14 group of breakaway hits but across the annual charts. From 1960 to 1966, between one and four of the top five films every year were epics or musicals with roadshow releases, and they always took the top positions (see appendix 3). Their status as family entertainment was confirmed when those that were re-released after 1968 received 'G' ratings (with the exception of *Doctor Zhivago* and *The Bridge on the River Kwai*). From 1967, epics and musicals did not only disappear from the Top 14 group of breakaway hits, but they also were, with few exceptions, sliding down the annual charts, and, what is more, they were less family-oriented, as is indicated by their more restrictive ratings. While a more detailed account of the ratings system will be provided later to determine the shifting meanings of the various categories, for the time being ratings are used as a rough-and-ready indicator of the intended and actual audiences for films.

The highest-ranked musicals of 1967 were the animated *The Jungle Book* at no. 4 and *Thoroughly Modern Millie* at no. 10. In terms of chart rankings, 1968 and 1969 were still good years for musicals, with the Fanny Brice biopic *Funny Girl* (1st/1968), the Charles Dickens and Broadway adaptation *Oliver!* (6th/1968; also the winner of the Best Picture and Best Director Oscars), Barbra Streisand's follow-up to *Funny Girl*, *Hello, Dolly!* (5th/1969), and the musical western *Paint Your Wagon* (7th/1969). While 1970 was a lean year, musicals were back in the top ten in 1971: *Fiddler on the Roof* was the top-grossing film of the year, and Disney's *Bedknobs and Broomsticks* came in at no. 10. 1972 had *Cabaret* (no. 6) and the biopic of black blues singer Billie Holliday, *Lady Sings the Blues* (no. 10), yet these musicals were no longer traditional family entertainment. Whereas all of the hit musicals from 1967 to 1971 (with the exception of *Paint Your Wagon*) were rated 'G' during their original release or their first re-release, *Cabaret* was a 'PG' (due to its sexual content, it could easily have been an 'R') and *Lady Sings the Blues* an 'R'. After two years' absence from the top ten, the musical returned in 1975, mainly in a different musical idiom. In addition to the traditional showtunes of the *Funny Girl* sequel *Funny Lady* (8th/1975, 'PG'), there were the rock opera *Tommy* (10th/1975, 'PG') and *A Star is Born* (2nd/1976, 'R'), the second remake of a classic movie, this time

FIGURE 5 *Funny Girl* (William Wyler, 1968)

as a fictional pop and rock biopic. Furthermore, unlike most of the earlier hit musicals, these films were no longer given a roadshow release. Thus, traditional musicals lost ground in the late 1960s and then largely disappeared from the top ten after 1971, while youth-oriented musicals, which were no longer presented as special events and had more 'mature' content perceived to be unsuitable for children, became ever more successful (a trend that continued after 1976, as we will see in the conclusion).

Two of the hit musicals had distinctly epic qualities: *Cabaret*'s love story was set against the rise of fascism, while the story of *Fiddler on the Roof* culminated with the mass emigration of Jews from the pogrom-ridden Russian Empire. Apart from these two, few films in the top ten tackled important developments in Western history directly and in an epically spectacular fashion. The Biblical epic – which had still provided the no. 2

hit of 1966, *The Bible: In the Beginning* – disappeared altogether from the annual top ten, replaced, one might argue, by 'R'-rated films about satanic possession which had epic resonances yet were presented as intimate relationship or family dramas (*Rosemary's Baby*, 7th/1968; *The Exorcist*, 1st/1973; *The Omen*, 6th/1976). Non-religious epics occasionally appeared in the top ten, but never again as high as *Gone With the Wind* (2nd/1967; rated 'G' during another re-release in 1971). Most of them were Second World War movies – with the boundaries between epics and more narrowly focused combat films being fluid – in the tradition of *The Bridge on the River Kwai*, *The Guns of Navarone* and *The Longest Day*. They tended to feature ensemble casts on more or less important war missions, and to place a particular emphasis both on the brutality of war and its procedural dimension. These films, most of which were very expensive and given roadshow releases, included *The Dirty Dozen* (6th/1967), *M*A*S*H* (3rd/1970), *Patton* (4th/1970; also the main Oscar winner of 1970, with an almost clean sweep of the major categories), *Tora! Tora! Tora!* (8th/1970), *Catch-22* (9th/1970) and, after a long break, *Midway* (10th/1976). *The Dirty Dozen*, *M*A*S*H* and *Catch-22* stand out from this group and from the Second World War epic tradition, due to their cynicism and strong sense of absurdity. The first one was never given a rating, the others initially received an 'R', while the more traditional *Tora! Tora! Tora!* was a 'G', *Midway* a 'PG' and *Patton* a 'M' ('suggested for mature audiences', a transitional category about which more will be said below).

The few hit epics not about the Second World War also moved away from 'G'-ratings. *Little Big Man* (6th/1970), the only one of the westerns in the annual top ten which had true epic scope, while at the same time offering a revisionist, often absurd and in places extremely brutal perspective on American history, received a 'GP'. *Ryan's Daughter* (7th/1970), the only epic romance in the annual top ten apart from *Gone With the Wind*, was initially given an 'R', but received a 'GP' on appeal. The two science fiction epics *2001: A Space Odyssey* (2nd/1968) and *Planet of the Apes* (7th/1968) were both rated 'G', but the former was far from child-friendly. Thus, from 1967 to 1970 traditional family-oriented roadshow epics, lost ground to war films, westerns and science fiction movies which were less suitable or altogether unsuitable for children, and after 1970 all variants of the epic disappeared from the top ten (except for *Midway*), a decline even more drastic than for traditional musicals.

These shifts were mainly caused by changes in film production, whereas, as we will see below, audience support for traditional epics and musicals remained remarkably strong. Let us first take a closer look at the period 1967–1971 when family-oriented roadshows still had a strong presence in the annual charts, best exemplified by their ability to take one of the two top spots in 1967, 1968 and 1971, with both *Gone With the Wind* and *Fiddler on the Roof* having earnings comparable to those of the New Hollywood Top 14. It is somewhat ironic that the main reason for the failure of other roadshow epics and musicals to match the breakaway success of *Gone With the Wind* and *Fiddler on the Roof* was overproduction; the roadshow format became a victim of its own success (see Hall 1999: vol. 1, 439–42).

Due to the extraordinary box office earnings of many roadshows, the number of films being presented in this fashion (many of them traditional musicals and epics, although more and more youth-oriented movies and art films were roadshown as well) had steadily increased over the years. Their number grew from one or two per year in the late 1940s and 1950s to about ten per year in the first half of the 1960s and between 15 and 20 in the second half (see Hall 1999: vol. 2, 36–92). Furthermore, several of the successful roadshows of the mid-1960s stayed in theatres for years, thus further increasing the number of roadshows on release in the second half of the decade. This substantial increase undermined the very specialness which was the distinguishing feature and main attraction of roadshows. At the same time, roadshowing youth-oriented and even art films undermined the long-standing assocation of the roadshow format with family entertainment (Hall 1999: vol. 1, 13, 304–10).

As noted above, traditionally, roadshows were presented as big family events, which, in addition to appealing to regular cinemagoers, were addressed to the large number of people who had lost the cinemagoing habit and would only go to the movies on special occasions. When the number of such special occasions grew across the 1960s, attendance of infrequent cinemagoers did not rise accordingly. Instead it seems that they tended to pick one or two films from the roadshows on offer, thus spreading themselves across several films and reducing the number of tickets sold for each one. Audience surveys support this speculation. A 1957 survey found that of all Americans over 14, 39 per cent attended cinemas less than three times a year (Jowett 1976: 478). By the early 1970s, this percentage had not decreased – with a decrease indicating that those groups who had attended infrequently now went to the movies more often to see more road-shows – but it had in fact *increased* considerably. In 1972 and 1973, over 50 per cent of all Americans over 11 went to the cinema less than three times a year, which included a large proportion of Americans who said they never went at all (40 per cent in 1972 and 37 per cent in 1973) (Jowett 1976: 486; Gertner 1978: 32A). As a group, infrequent cinemagoers could still turn a roadshow into a breakaway hit (as they did with *Gone With the Wind* and *Fiddler on the Roof*), but, having so many roadshows to choose from, this was becoming much less likely. (Furthermore, as we will see later, women, who constituted a key audience for traditional roadshows, were one of the groups being alienated from cinemagoing in the late 1960s.)

The declining number of breakaway roadshow hits was not the only consequence of overproduction. Production costs had risen so much during the 1960s that many roadshow releases required breakaway success to be profitable (Hall 1999: vol. 1, 236–41). Anything less caused losses, even if the film in question made it into the annual top ten (an early, and extreme, example of a top hit losing money is *Cleopatra*). For instance, *Hello, Dolly!* (5th/1969) earned $15.2m in rentals but it cost $25.3m to make (excluding the substantial costs for prints and advertising); the figures for *Tora! Tora! Tora!* (8th/1970) were $14.5m and $25.5m respectively (1999: vol. 1, 238). Other roadshow releases from this period made even less money in the US. The musical *Star!* (1968) earned $4.2m in rentals against a budget of $14.3m, while the Second World War epic *Battle of Britain* (1969) had US rentals of $2m and a budget of $14m, and the musical *Darling Lili* (1970) earned $3.3m against a budget of $16.7m (ibid.). It would seem that the disastrous performance of such films in the US was, to some extent, mir-rored by the declining success of roadshow epics and musicals abroad. In Germany, one of the largest foreign markets, for example, Hollywood epics had regularly ranked in the annual top ten, but – with the exception of *Battle of Britain* (no. 9 in the 1969/70 season) – they stopped doing so after *Doctor Zhivago* (the top hit of 1966/67) (Garncarz 1994: 124–31). Thus, losses in the domestic market could not be recouped abroad. Indeed, the losses incurred by superexpensive roadshow musicals and epics were probably the main reason for the enormous overall corporate losses several of the major studios suffered in 1969 and 1970 (Finler 1988: 286–7; Hall 1999: vol. 1, 236–40).

After the near-catastrophe of 1969/70, the major studios finally changed direction, drastically reducing the number of roadshow releases so that by 1973 they had virtually disappeared. It is important to note that this change in industry strategy did *not* in any direct way reflect a diminishing taste for traditional roadshows on the part of Americans. Indeed, in addition to the solid US box office performance of many traditional roadshow epics and musicals until 1971, there is plenty of evidence that across the decade 1967–76 Americans continued to favour these kinds of films. To begin with, five of the Roadshow Era Top 14, including four epics and musicals – *Ben-Hur* (broadcast in 1971), *The Sound of Music* (1976), *The Ten Commandments* (1973) and *The Robe* (1967) (the fifth film was *Goldfinger*, 1972) – achieved ratings over 30 when they were broadcast during this decade, and *The Bridge on the River Kwai* had a 38 rating in 1966 (Steinberg 1980: 32–3). As of 1976, four of these films were among the twenty top-rated theatrical movies ever shown on television (and only two made-for-TV movies did equally well); they sat right next to many of the New Hollywood Top 14 in this chart (1980: 32). It is also worth noting that when *Ben-Hur* was first broadcast in 1971, it became the second-highest-rated theatrical movie in American television history up to this point – after *The Bridge on the River Kwai* (ibid.).

Roadshow Era superhits also did extremely well in audience polls. When, in 1970, the *Los Angeles Times* asked readers for the best film of the 1960s, *The Sound of Music*, *West Side Story*, *Doctor Zhivago* and *My Fair Lady* were among the top ten, which, as mentioned earlier, was led by *The Graduate* (Steinberg 1980: 145). Seven years later, the *Los Angeles Times* again asked its readers for their favourites, and both *The Sound of Music* and *Ben-Hur* made it into the top twenty, right next to *One Flew Over the Cuckoo's Nest* and *The Graduate* (1980: 189). One might suspect that older respondents in these polls voted for the Roadshow Era films while youth voted for those of the New Hollywood, but this was not necessarily the case. A 1978 poll of college students found that *The Sound of Music* was their third favourite film, just ahead of *Rocky* (1980: 183).

The film industry and critics also continued to embrace many of the Roadshow Era Top 14. In the 1970 *Los Angeles Times* poll, filmmakers considered *The Sound of Music* one of the ten best films of the 1960s, while once again *The Graduate* was considered the very best (1980: 146). The University of Southern California's 1972 panel of filmmakers and critics included the following on its list of the fifty most significant American films of all time: *West Side Story*, *The Bridge on the River Kwai*, *The Sound of Music*, *Ben-Hur* and *The Robe*; from the New Hollywood Top 14 they included *The Godfather* as well as *The Graduate* (Steinberg 1980: 187). A 1975 poll of top film and television executives listed *My Fair Lady* among their thirty favourite films, but none of the New Hollywood Top 14 (1980: 186). Finally, the 1977 AFI membership poll found *Ben-Hur*, *The Bridge on the River Kwai*, *The Sound of Music* and *West Side Story* in the top fifty, together with seven of the New Hollywood Top 14 (1980: 144).

Thus, after 1966, American film industry personnel, critics and movie audiences continued to appreciate and even love the superhits of the Roadshow Era. Some of the films had successful re-releases in the cinema, most notably *The Sound of Music* and *Mary Poppins* in 1973 (Steinberg 1980: 27). Indeed, through extended runs into the late 1960s and re-releases in the early 1970s, both *The Sound of Music* and *Doctor Zhivago* (re-released in 1971/72) earned over \$30m in rentals from 1967 to 1976, thus joining the ranks of the decade's biggest hits (see appendix 1). However, the most spectacular re-release of an old-style epic superhit was that of *Gone With the Wind* in 1967/68. Somewhat perversely, the \$36m which the film generated in rentals during its roadshow release at this time and during another re-release in 1971/72 might even qualify it to be included in the New Hollywood Top 14. What is more, in almost every conceivable way, *Gone With the Wind* was the most outstanding film in American culture during the period 1967–76. It was first shown on TV in two parts in 1976 with astronomical ratings over 47; even today it is by far the highest-rated theatrical movie on television ever (1980: 32). Indeed in 1976, it was the highest-rated programme of any kind in American television history up to this point (it is still in the top ten today) (*People* 2000: 162). Several polls conducted during this period found that *Gone With the Wind* was also by far the favourite movie of Americans (1980: 183, 189), even among college students and – despite the film's close association with female audiences – among older educated males (Anon. 1970). Furthermore, *Gone With the Wind* came out on top in some polls of critics and film industry personnel as the best American movie ever (Steinberg 1980: 144, 182, 187).

Since *Gone With the Wind* and the Roadshow Era superhits remained absolutely central to American film culture from 1967 to 1976, Hollywood's abandonment of traditional roadshows in the early 1970s was by no means a response to declining audience demand. Instead, we can understand this abandonment as the major studios' belated and overly drastic reaction to the huge roadshow losses of 1969/70. It also was a reaction to their success with other, cheaper types of films. Most prominent amongst them were youth-oriented taboo-breakers and family-oriented disaster movies.

The rise of taboo-breakers

Mainstream hits breaking with the American film industry's long-standing restraint on matters of sex and violence as well as other controversial subjects became possible once Hollywood's Production Code was fatally weakened in 1966. The Production Code had originally been adopted in 1930 by the major studios' trade organisation – the Motion Picture Producers and Distributors of America, later renamed Motion Picture Association of America (MPAA) – to ensure that films shown in mainstream movie theatres followed certain guidelines. These were intended to make sure, as much as that was possible, that all films were basically suitable for all audiences, including children, and that, furthermore, film screenings would not provoke public controversy and official intervention through municipal or state censorship or even new legislation. Censorship and new legislation were bound to complicate the industry's operations, increasing costs along the way. While controversy might make the film in question more appealing, it could damage the reputation of the film industry as a whole and alienate certain segments of the population from the cinemagoing experience altogether. The Code was enforced by the MPAA's Production Code Adminstration (PCA), which reviewed all scripts for American productions as well as prints of films (of both American and foreign origin) to be given a mainstream release, and, if necessary, negotiated changes to bring films into line with the Code's guidelines. While a few films – mostly European imports and exploitation films – were shown without the PCA's Seal of Approval, these were seen by comparatively few people and on the whole remained economically marginal (on the limited success of foreign language films, see Anon. 1991a).

The Code was framed by 'general principles' such as: 'No picture shall be produced which will lower the moral standards of those who see it', and 'law, natural or human, shall not be ridiculed, nor shall sympathy be created for its violation' (Steinberg 1980: 391). Specific stipulations concerned the representation of violent acts – for example, 'brutal killings are not to be presented in detail' – and of sexuality: 'adultery and illicit sex ... must not be explicitly treated or justified, or treated attractively'; 'excessive and lustful kissing, lustful embraces, suggestive postures and gestures are not to be shown', certainly 'not to stimulate the lower and baser emotions' (1980: 392). With further restrictions, for example, on nudity, profanity and criticisms of religion, it is easy to see that much of what was shown from 1966 onwards had simply not been possible in a mainstream release before that time. What is more, the Catholic Church had exerted enormous pressure on Hollywood through its Legion of Decency until the liberalisation of the Church in the early to mid-1960s (Walsh 1996; Black 1998). Finally, censorship boards had continued operating for a while after official censorship by federal states and municipalities had been declared unconstitutional when film (except for cases of extreme 'obscenity') was included under the Constitution's protection of free speech in 1952, yet in the early 1960s these boards were finally being phased out (see Jowett 1996).

By 1966, then, the necessity and usefulness of the Production Code, which had always been subject to some debate, was becoming ever more doubtful. When a major row between Warner Bros., the Legion of Decency and the PCA erupted during the production of *Who's Afraid of Virginia Woolf?* (1966), an adaptation of a recent play featuring Elizabeth Taylor and Richard Burton as a married couple involved in vicious verbal fights with plenty of profanity and obscenity, Warner Bros. decided to release the film with the warning 'No One Under 18 Admitted Without Parent' (see Leff & Simmons 1990: 241–66; Black 1998: 229–32; Walsh 1996: 312–3). Rather than insisting on changes which would bring the film in line with the Production Code, the PCA accepted Warner Bros.' label and approved the film, which went on to become the third-highest-grossing film of 1966. Soon after the *Who's Afraid of Virginia Woolf?* decision, in September 1966, the new president of the MPAA, Jack Valenti, revealed a brand-new Production Code. This, in effect, removed most prohibitions because it allowed for the possibility that particularly challenging films could be released with the label 'suggested for mature audiences'. It soon turned out that the majority of films approved by the PCA carried this label, making nonsense of the Code (Leff & Simmons 1990: 270). When two Supreme Court decisions in the spring of 1968 opened up the possibility that states and cities would replace censorship with ratings, which stipulated the age range of audiences allowed to attend particular films in that state or city, the MPAA quickly moved to institute its own ratings system, partly to avoid an unmanageable patchwork of regional age restrictions (Steinberg 1980: 399–401). On 1 November 1968, the PCA was replaced with the Code and Rating Administration (CARA), which reviewed all scripts and finished films and negotiated with studios about the changes they might have to make to get a desired rating.

The 'G' rating was initially set up as a continuation of the pre-1966 Production Code, being given to films which were deemed suitable for all audiences. Indeed, the vast majority of pre-1966 movies that were re-released from 1968 onwards were given 'G' ratings. However, as we have seen, four of the Roadshow Era Top 14 were re-released with 'GP'/'PG' ratings, and several other hits also received non-'G' ratings, most notably *Psycho* (2nd/1960) which was rated 'M' in 1968 and 'R' in 1984. The meaning of all ratings was in flux in the late 1960s and early 1970s. Within a few years 'G' was rarely used and rather than signifying a film's acceptability for both young and old, it was soon widely understood to refer to films which were in effect *only* suitable for children (Krämer 2002b: 191; Steinberg 1980: 399–404). The 'M' rating was equivalent to the 'suggested for mature audiences' label so popular from 1966 to 1968; indeed 'M' immediately became the most frequently used rating. However, there was considerable confusion about whether 'M' was meant to signal that films were unsuitable for children due to their mature content, or whether these films might be appropriate for children after all. Changing 'M' into 'GP' ('parental guidance suggested') in 1970, and then into 'PG' in 1972, made it clear that films so rated were child-friendly, despite some mature elements. The 'R' rating, which quickly became almost as popular as 'M', required that children under 16 be accompanied by an adult, and the very rarely used 'X' excluded those children altogether and became increasingly associated with pornography. In 1970, the age limit for 'R' and 'X' was raised to 17.

The upshot of all these developments was that, from 1966 onwards, mainstream hits breaking long-established taboos became possible, which in turn exerted a strong influence on future production patterns and audience decisions. The influence of such hits derived both from their box office performance and the intense, often controversial public debate they generated. Let us take a look at the breakthrough hits of 1967. While sex was highlighted in the poster for *The Graduate* and in many reviews (see, for example, Elley 2000: 337), the film did not generate much controversy. John Simon of *The New Leader* disliked it, but mentioned only in passing that 'a few taboos are, indeed, broken' (1968: 30). There was great excitement and disagreement among critics and among audience members, as evidenced by the many letters debating the film's merits in the *New York Times* months after it had first been shown, yet this appeared to concern the film's 'arty' style and the effectiveness of its satire more than its representation of sexuality. Nevertheless, the breakaway success of *The Graduate* exerted a strong influence when it came to sexually-themed films. Explicit depictions of highly unusual romantic entanglements and sexual practices in contemporary American settings could now become mainstream entertainment. Before 1967 such representations had been less frequent, less explicit and often confined to historical settings, as, for example, in *Cleopatra* (1st/1963) and *Tom Jones* (3rd/1963), the most notable exception among major hits being the Bond films, which were, however, far removed from the realities of contemporary American life.

In the wake of *The Graduate*, extensive displays of nudity, men cavorting with prostitutes or prostituting themselves, married middle-class couples contemplating partner swaps, prostitutes featured as comic heroines, men sleeping around in search not of love but of sexual gratification, and extra-marital affairs between older women and young men could be found in many films set in contemporary America, including the following top ten hits: *Midnight Cowboy* (3rd/1969, rated 'X'), *Easy Rider* (4th/1969, 'R'), *Bob & Carol & Ted & Alice* (6th/1969, 'R'), *Woodstock* (5th/1970, 'R'), *The Owl and the Pussycat* (10th/1970, 'R'), *The French Connection* (3rd/1971, 'R'), *Carnal Knowledge* (8th/1971, 'R') and *The Last Picture Show* (9th/1971, 'R', set in the recent past). Just outside the top ten, there were sexually explicit films such as the Swedish import *I am Curious: Yellow* (with $8.5m rentals in 1969, belatedly rated 'X' in 1973) and Russ Meyer's *Beyond the Valley of the Dolls* ($7m, 1970, 'X') (see Cohn 1993).

This trend culminated with the surprising success of 'X'-rated films in 1972 and 1973, when both the Euro-American art film *Last Tango in Paris* (7th/1973), with its graphically portrayed, extensive and in places violent sexual acts (including, famously, anal penetration), and the hardcore porn movies *Deep Throat* (7th/1972) and *The Devil in Miss Jones* (10th/1973) achieved top ten success (see Lewis 2000: ch. 5). The extremes of 1972/73 were not replicated in later years, at least not in hit movies. Indeed, sexual themes and the graphic depiction of sexual acts became generally much less important in the annual top ten – with some notable exceptions such as the sexually hyperactive hairdresser in *Shampoo* (3rd/1975, 'R'), the bi-sexual bank robber who wants to finance his boyfriend's sex change operation in *Dog Day Afternoon* (4th/1975, 'R') and the extensive sex scenes in *A Star is Born* (2nd/1976, 'R').

Going back to 1967, I have already noted that this was the breakthrough year for extremely violent films with *Bonnie and Clyde* (5th/1967, rated 'M' in 1969) and *The Dirty Dozen* (6th/1967). Both films also featured extensive scenes dealing with sex (in the former mainly revolving around the woman's arousal and the man's inability to perform, in the latter involving prostitutes), which in some instances explored the connection between sex and violence (as when Bonnie Parker is aroused by Clyde Barrow's robbery of a store). It is not altogether surprising that, after 1967, violent sex and sexualised violence became a feature of top-ten movies (also, of course, of many movies outside the top ten such as *Straw Dogs*, 1971). However, these were often set outside contemporary America. The most notable examples come in the early 1970s. In what is arguably the most shocking scene of *A Clockwork Orange* (7th/1971, 'X', changed to 'R' in 1972), a film set in a futuristic Britain, a group of young men beat up a writer and force him to watch his wife being gang-raped, while their leader cheerfully intones 'Singin' in the Rain'. The story of *Deliverance* (4th/1972, 'R') revolves around one of the four river-rafting adventurers being raped by two local men. Then, 1973 saw the release not only of *Last Tango in Paris*, which blurred the lines between rape and consensual sex, but also of *The Exorcist* ('R'). In this film a twelve-year-old girl, possessed by a male-identified demon, spouts incredibly graphic obscenities (such as 'Your mother sucks cocks in hell') and mimicks sexual behaviour, most shockingly when she violently stabs her genitals with a bloody crucifix, doing so in front of her mother, whose face she then pushes into her crotch with the words 'Lick me!' An important precursor for such excess was a scene in *Rosemary's Baby* (7th/1968, 'R'), in which the drugged and only semi-conscious young wife is penetrated and inseminated by the Devil himself. Yet while there is this precursor for *The Exorcist*, there was no commercially successful attempt to replicate the extremes of its sexualised violence after 1973.

Sexual representations (both violent and non-violent) were clearly peaking in the box office charts of 1972/73. For non-sexual violence, it

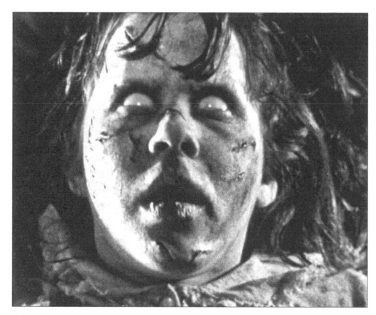

FIGURE 6 *The Exorcist* (William Friedkin, 1973)

is much less obvious whether such a peak exists. The two breakthrough hyperviolent films of 1967, *Bonnie and Clyde* and *The Dirty Dozen*, gener-ated enormous controversy, which linked them so closely to social unrest, assassinations and rising crime rates in American society that Hollywood's potential role in increasing levels of violence in the US became the focus of the National Commission on the Causes and Prevention of Violence in 1968 (see Prince 1998: 18–30 and 2000a: 47–75; Hoberman 1998; on the diverse and changing meanings of the term 'violence', see Prince 2003: 253–63, and Barker 2004). Building on the impact these two films had at the box office and in public debates, the annual charts after 1967 included numerous films featuring the large-scale destruction of property, often during protracted chase sequences, and high levels of interpersonal violence, frequently showing extremes of human suffering and graphically depicting the physical impact of such violence on the human body, so groundbreakingly shown in the climactic slow motion slaughter of Bonnie Parker and Clyde Barrow (see Prince 1998: ch. 2).

In addition to the war and disaster films discussed above and, of course, to Bond films which continued to populate the annual top ten, violent action of various types and levels of intensity (usually indicated by the rating) featured prominently in contemporary crime films including *Bullitt* (4th/1968, 'M'), *The French Connection* (3rd/1971, 'R'), *Dirty Harry* (6th/1971, 'R'), *The Getaway* (8th/1972, 'PG'), *Magnum Force* (6th/1973, 'R'), *Dog Day Afternoon* (4th/1975, 'R') and *The Enforcer* (8th/1976, 'R'); in contemporary dramas pitting countercultural protagonists against establishment figures like *Easy Rider* (4th/1969, 'R'), *Billy Jack* (2nd/1971, 'GP'), *The Trial of Billy Jack* (5th/1974, 'PG') and *One Flew Over the Cuckoo's Nest* (2nd/1975, 'R'); in adventure films like *Deliverance* (which, in addition to the rape, had prolonged scenes of men fighting the rapids as well as each other) and *Jaws* (1st/1975, 'PG'), and sports movies like *The Longest Yard* (8th/1974, 'R') and *Rocky* (1st/1976, 'PG'); in horror films such as *The Exorcist* (which, in addition to sexualised violence, also featured extreme violence both against adults and against the little girl) and *The Omen* (6th/1976, 'R', a film prominently featuring a father's attempt to kill his son); in science fiction films like *Planet of the Apes* (7th/1968, 'G') and *A Clockwork Orange* (which featured several brutal beatings in addition to rape); and in historical dramas like the westerns *Butch Cassidy and the Sundance Kid* (1st/1969, 'M'), *True Grit* (8th/1969, 'M'), *Little Big Man* (6th/1970, 'GP') and *Jeremiah Johnson* (5th/1972, 'GP'), the gangster films *The Godfather* (1st/1972, 'R') and *The Godfather, Part II* (6th/1974, 'R'), and the prison movie *Papillon* (4th/1973, 'R' changed to 'PG' after an appeal).

A lot of this violence could be characterised as criminal. Indeed a quantitative content analysis of a representative sample of hit movies showed that the share of major characters committing crimes rose from 27 per cent in the period 1946–65 to 46 per cent in the decade 1966–75; the share of major characters resorting to violence (both criminal and legal) doubled from 19 per cent to 38 per cent (Powers, Rothman & Rothman 1996: 105). The frequency of 'R' and 'M' ratings for the above films is the most clear-cut indication that from 1967 the annual top ten were focused to a much greater extent on violent representations than in preceding decades, and on more violent representations, including countless instances of damage to the human body that would not have been shown before at all (see Prince 2003). But unlike sexual representations, including sexual violence, there is no sense that non-sexual violence in hit movies was reaching its peak and then abating at any point during the early to mid-1970s.

One way to understand these developments is to assume a pent-up unsatisfied demand for sexual and violent cinematic representations, as well as other challenging depictions of contemporary reality, among a relatively small segment of the American population, mostly youth and especially males, with the majority of Americans clearly being opposed to such representations. Two 1968 surveys, for example, found that the majority of young people 'approve of the high degree of realism in film content that has taken place in recent years'; in particular, of those under 30 'only a small fraction have strong objections to increased emphasis on sex' or to more violence on the screen (Anon. 1968b; Warga 1968). Remarkably, a 1974 survey found that 10 per cent of males declared that 'X'-rated films were among their most preferred types of film (while both males, with 25 per cent, and females, with 43 per cent, also declared that 'X'-rated films were by far their *least* preferred type of film); action-oriented and increasingly violent genres such as westerns (22 per cent), suspense films (16 per cent) and war movies (9 per cent) also scored highly with males but much less so with females (Newspaper Advertising Bureau 1974).

Three films released in 1967 managed to meet this pent-up demand and become major hits (*The Graduate* was, as we have seen, a true breakaway hit; its rentals were matched by the combined income of *Bonnie and Clyde* and *The Dirty Dozen*). This encouraged the film industry to invest more heavily in such movies, by making more of them, but also by making them more expensively, with *The Exorcist*, for example, costing $10m (Finler 2003: 298). Furthermore, the Academy of Motion Picture Arts and Sciences gave taboo-breaking films an even higher profile by awarding them plenty of Oscars; *Midnight Cowboy* and *The French Connection*, for example, won Best Picture and Best Director for 1969 and 1971 respectively. In the light of Hollywood's increasing investments in, and publicity for, such challenging films, people who had liked the three breakthrough hits of 1967 were encouraged to come back for, among other things, more sexual and violent attractions, which also probably aroused the curiosity of a wider range of people who had not seen the initial films. To some extent, their surprising, even shocking impact could be replicated only by intensifying the sexual and violent representations, which set in motion a process of escalation. In the case of sex and sexual violence, this process reached such extremes from 1971 to 1973 that people both in the film industry and in the audience who had supported this escalation eventually turned against it. Consequently, among top-ten hits both the number of films featuring explicit sex or sexual violence and the intensity of sexual representations declined. In the case of non-sexual violence, however, the escalation proceeded more slowly (at least in hit movies; in the low-budget horror sector it arguably matched the sexual extremes of the hits of 1971–73), so that this violence could gradually become a new standard rather than an exceptional attraction.

Race relations were another sensitive aspect of contemporary American reality which hits from 1967 onwards began to address in new ways, with the result that African-Americans could become a standard part of cinematic entertainment by 1976. Once again a major controversial hit of 1967 prepared the way for more extensive and diverse representations in hit movies (see Bogle 1997: chs. 7–8). *Guess Who's Coming to Dinner* (3rd/1967) starred Spencer Tracy (who died shortly after filming stopped), Sidney Poitier and Katherine Hepburn in a drama about the difficulties of white liberal parents to accept their daughter's impending marriage to a black man. Arthur Knight (1967) wrote in the *Saturday Review* that the film broke new ground insofar as it was the first major studio release 'to give serious attention to the question of interracial marriage – or even to permit a Negro male enthusiastically to kiss a white female'. Although some reviewers felt that the film was too stagey, all too tasteful and atypical in its social setting, the majority welcomed the fact that it treated an important social issue in an entertaining and apparently inoffensive fashion (see, for example, Elley 2000: 348). However, a look at the extensive racist hate mail which producer-director Stanley Kramer received from the moment his film project was announced, suggests that, outside mainstream media, the film was surrounded by great controversy (the letters are contained in the Stanley Kramer Papers, Special Collections, Theater Arts Library, University of California at Los Angeles).

Guess Who's Coming to Dinner was not the only hit of 1967 dealing with race. Indeed, race was an important issue in half of the top ten hits that year, which is perhaps not so surprising in the context of ongoing heated debates about Civil Rights, the emergence of the Black Power movement and the formation of the Black Panther party in 1966 as well as a series of major race riots from 1965 to 1967. Hits with racial themes included the re-released Civil War epic *Gone With the Wind* (2nd/1967) and the latest Disney animation, *The Jungle Book* (4th/1967). This film tells the story of the human orphan Mowgli who has to return from the jungle to his own (human) kind, because ultimately he is racially incompatible with the animals who have raised him and is hated by Shere Khan, the tiger, simply for being human. Quite problematically, the film also depicts monkeys as dwellers in a jungle ghetto associated with black musical forms. Furthermore, *The Dirty Dozen* (6th/1967) prominently featured African-American football star Jim Brown. Most impressive, however, was the box office dominance of Sidney Poitier. In addition to *Guess Who's Coming to Dinner*, he starred in *To Sir, With Love* (at no. 9), a drama about a black school teacher in London, as well as *In the Heat of the Night*, a film about a black police detective who, during a visit in the deep South, is suspected of murder and then goes on to solve the crime, in the process giving an offensive Southern aristocrat a memorable slap in the face and earning the respect of the racist local sheriff. While *In the Heat of the Night* (with rentals of $11m; Cohn 1993) was placed just outside the top ten, it won five Oscars, including Best Picture. As a result of these three hits, Poitier became the first black performer ever to be ranked among Quigley's top ten box office attractions. He was at no. 7 in 1967 and, since his three 1967 films had long runs into 1968, was designated the biggest movie star in the US in 1968, before slipping down to no. 6 in 1969 and disappearing from the top ten thereafter (Steinberg 1980: 60).

In the following years, racial themes and African-American performers were central to a wide range of films, including, in the first half of the 1970s (especially in 1972–4), dozens of mostly low-budget action films with predominantly black casts (so-called 'blaxploitation' films), which were addressed primarily to African-Americans and rarely crossed over to white audiences (see Cook 2000: 259–66). With the exception of the hardboiled private eye thriller *Shaft* (1971, $7m rentals) and the drug dealer drama *Super Fly* (1972, $6.4m) (Cohn 1993), such films did not even come close to the annual top ten. However, top ten hits also continued to address racial issues. Across all hit movies, the share of (major and minor) characters belonging to a racial minority (Black, Asian, Native American or Hispanic) doubled from 5.5 per cent for 1946–65 to 11 per cent for 1966–75 (Powers, Rothman & Rothman 1996: 175). *Planet of the Apes* (7th/1968) presented an allegory of contemporary American race relations (see Greene 1998), while racial prejudice and racially motivated violence were also explored with reference to Native Americans in *Little Big Man* (6th/1970), *Billy Jack* (2nd/1971) and *The Trial of Billy Jack* (5th/1974). *Woodstock* (5th/1970) prominently featured black musicians, most notably Jimi Hendrix (whose *Are You Experienced?* had been the top-selling album of 1968), and *Lady Sings the Blues* (10th/1972) told the story of a blues legend, played by pop star Diana Ross (who had had a string of hit singles and albums, both on her own and as a member of the Supremes, since the mid-1960s) (*People* 2000: 219–20, 224). In *Magnum Force* (6th/1973) 'Dirty' Harry Callahan gets a black partner, and in *Live and Let Die* (9th/1973) James Bond fights black gangsters. *The Towering Inferno* (1st/1974) featured former football star O. J. Simpson in its all-star cast, and *Earthquake* (4th/1974) Richard Roundtree – who had risen to stardom with *Shaft* (1971), in which he constantly crossed the barriers between racial communities, among other things having sex with a white woman. While none of these black performers were included in Quigley's annual list of the top ten box office attractions, their potential drawing power was recognised by their inclusion in Quigley's annual 'Stars of Tomorrow' list: Jim Brown was listed in 1968, Richard Roundtree in 1971, Ron O'Neal (from *Super Fly*) in 1972 and Diana Ross in 1973 (Steinberg 1980: 64–5).

These trends culminated in the breakaway success of *Blazing Saddles* (2nd/1974, 'R'), a western parody about a black sheriff and his fight against corrupt white businessmen and politicians, featuring plenty of comically-rendered racial slurs and racially-motivated violence, but also a utopian vision of interracial alliances, including a sexual relationship between the black hero and a white woman. While building on earlier, racially-themed hits, *Blazing Saddles* also consolidated the most successful formula for future treatments of black/white relations: the bi-racial comedy-action team (here played by Cleavon Little and Gene Wilder). The first inkling of the ongoing success of this formula was provided by *Silver Streak* (4th/1976) which started out as a Gene Wilder comedy and then turned into an extended comedy routine between Wilder and black comedian Richard Pryor (who had co-written *Blazing Saddles*). Thus, by the mid-1970s, racial themes and African-American performers had become a standard – rather than a controversial – element of a range of hit movies. Indeed, from 1976 onwards, their share of (major and minor) characters was close to their

FIGURE 7 *Blazing Saddles* (Mel Brooks, 1974)

share of the American population; African-Americans were no longer under-represented (Powers, Rothman & Rothman 1996: 175).

The initially shocking breakthrough presentation of taboo subject matter in 1967, the escalation of the late 1960s and early 1970s, and the normalisation of such subject matter (either through its de-escalation or through its widespread acceptance) in the mid-1970s, exerted a strong influence on the composition of the American cinema audience across this decade.

The break-up and reconstitution of the family audience

The most pertinent fact about cinemagoing in this period was that a substantial number of Americans simply did not do it any longer. In 1972, when the escalation of violent, sexual and racial representations was nearing its peak, 40 per cent of Americans over 11, and 43 per cent of those over 17, said in a survey conducted for the MPAA that they never went to the cinema (Jowett 1976: 486; the survey did not cover young children). Non-attendance rates were highest among the people with the least income (60 per cent, as compared to 21 per cent for high earners) and those with little education (66 per cent, as compared to 20 per cent for the best educated); except for teenagers, they were higher for women than for men (1976: 485–6). If we also consider those who went only once or twice a year, the combined percentages for non-attenders and infrequent cinemagoers among various groups were as follows: 61 per cent of women over 17 versus 45 per cent of men over 17; 70 per cent of those earning less $7,000 versus 37 per cent of those earning $15,000 and more; 79 per cent of Americans without a high school diploma versus 36 per cent of those who had some higher education. Similarly extreme imbalances existed with respect to different age groups. Although people aged 30 and over made up 61 per cent of the American population over 11, they accounted for only 27 per cent of ticket purchases; attendance levels declined with age, dropping dramatically at age 50. People under 30 accounted for 73 per cent of ticket purchases, while they made up only 39 per cent of the American population over 11.

While these imbalances had a long history, they had been intensifying over the years. For example, a 1957 survey (this time including children up to the age of 11) found that men went to the cinema slightly more often than women, that the lowest income group went less often than the highest income group (although, unlike in 1972, medium income groups were the most avid cinemagoers), and attendance increased with education (although the effect of higher education was less pronounced than in 1972) (Jowett 1976: 476–7). Those under 30 bought 72 per cent of all tickets, while they made up only 50 per cent of the population. This is not directly comparable to the 1972 figures because the latter excluded children under 12, but, by and large, there is once again a strong bias towards youth, although it is less pronounced than in 1972. The drop-off in the frequency of cinema attendance at the age of 30 was certainly much less dramatic in 1957 than it was in 1972.

In trying to understand the increasing dominance of the youth audience, we can first of all note demographic changes. The most avid cinemagoers in 1957 were 15–19-year-olds (making up only 7 per cent of the population but accounting for 21 per cent of all ticket purchases), followed by 20–29-year-olds (9 per cent/15 per cent) and 10–14-year-olds (12 per cent/20 per cent); furthermore, 20–24-year-olds tended to go to the cinema more frequently than 25–29-year-olds (Jowett 1976: 477, 485). Due to the postwar baby boom (that is the increased birthrates between 1946 and 1964), the number of 15–24-year-olds, who were precisely the most avid cinemagoers, expanded considerably across the 1960s. In 1957, there were 22.3m people in this age group, making up 13 per cent of the US population; in 1970, there were 36.5m, accounting for 18 per cent of the population (Wattenberg 1976: 10). This goes a long way towards explaining why the concentration of ticket sales on the youth audience was much more pronounced in the early 1970s.

However, demographics cannot explain why the differences in the frequency of cinema attendances between those under 30 and those 30 and older, between men and women, between the well-educated and the uneducated, between the well-off and the poor increased so much from 1957 to 1972. In other words, what led to the relative reduction in attendance levels among women, older people, the poor and the uneducated, and what caused the relative increase in attendance levels among educated, middle-class male youth? I am not going to deal with income and educational differences (their extraordinary impact deserves a separate investigation), but I want to make some suggestions about the increasing differences along the lines of gender and age.

First of all, across the postwar period, industry observers and survey respondents had increasingly expressed the opinion that the film industry was not catering sufficiently to 'general' or family audiences – despite the fact that the PCA was meant to ensure that the vast majority of films released in the US were suitable for all segments of the population, including children. It seems that people were no longer convinced that PCA approval of a film guaranteed its suitability for children, and instead of expecting that all of Hollywood's output was in effect family entertainment, 'family films' emerged as a separate category. Thus, the *Christian Science Monitor* wrote: 'In recent years the clamour has increased for Hollywood to make more family films' (Anon. 1962). While there was some debate about how one might define this category, 'most people who speak about a family film mean one that does not deal with sex at all, or deals with it only in a negative definition' (ibid.).

The mutual exclusiveness of sex and family films was the main result of a 1967 survey by *McCall's* magazine among its female readers. While their favorite recent movies (*The Sound of Music*, *Doctor Zhivago* and *My*

Fair Lady) were described as 'family films', the list of 'least-liked' films was headed by *Who's Afraid of Virginia Woolf?*, and 'more than two-thirds said they were "almost always" or sometimes offended by "sex scenes or overly frank dialogue"', because these were 'out of step with their personal and parental attitudes' (Anon. 1967a). Concerns about Hollywood's departure from family entertainment, then, were closely connected to the age and gender of respondents, with mothers being particularly affected. The MPAA acknowledged such concerns in February 1968 when its president, Jack Valenti, declared that the film industry's 'single most outstanding weakness ... lies in its failures to meet the demands of young married couples with children' (Anon. 1968a). Yet with the total removal of the Production Code that year, worries about the provision of child-friendly family entertainment only increased. A 1970 poll revealed 'widespread dissatisfaction with available children's fare' among 68 per cent of all respondents (Wolf 1970). Two years later, Jerry Lewis (1972) headed an article in *Variety*: 'Children, Too Have Film Rights'. A 1974 survey found that 76 per cent of respondents said that there were not enough 'family pictures' (Anon. 1974a).

People were not just worried about children, though. Many, especially those over 30 (see Warga 1968) and women, were concerned about their own cinema experiences. Surveys in the early to mid-1960s had clearly identified what kind of experience most Americans were looking for in the cinema. In general, they preferred '(i) escapism to harsh reality, (ii) action to "talkiness", (iii) a happy ending, not without some sense of logic, (iv) relaxing rather than provocative themes, (v) glossy comedies to harsh tragedies, and (vi) a touch of "naughtiness", but never dirt for dirt's sake or violence for violence's sake' (Anon. 1963). Similarly, a 1964 survey identified 'a definite preference for entertainment which the entire family can enjoy ... Audiences want to escape – not be exposed to unappetising realities' (Anon. 1964). In the late 1960s and early 1970s, older Americans and women had many reasons to object to the amount of sex and violence and other problematic realities appearing on screen, also to the focus of many films on young and on male protagonists, and to the poor state of repair of many movie theatres (Krämer 1999: 85–7). In the 1974 survey quoted above, 52 per cent of respondents – probably mostly women and older people – agreed that 'sex, violence, or a combination of these ingredients keep people away' from the cinema (Anon. 1974a). Another 1974 survey listed the 'pet peeves of the 18–30 female audience': 'seats are too small, prices too high, theatres are dirty ... too hot or too cold, audiences are too noisy' (Anon. 1974b). Such complaints contributed to the declining attendance levels among women and older people across the 1960s and the early 1970s.

At the same time, these groups, like everyone else, had become increasingly accustomed to watching films on television, turning, as we have seen, traditional roadshow epics and musicals into ratings champions. The popularity of films (both older and recent) on television is also suggested by the fact that in 1966/67, for the first time, NBC's *Saturday Night at the Movies* and the *CBS Friday Night Movies* were ranked among the twenty top-rated shows on television; for the next decade these and other 'movie nights' were regularly ranked in the top twenty (*People* 2000: 154–6). Apparently, women and older people felt much more comfortable watching films at home than venturing out to a movie theatre.

Here we find another reason for the rapid disappearance of family roadshows in the early 1970s. The alienation of women was particularly damaging for the chances of success of traditional musicals and of romantic historical epics. When asked about their preferred types of movies, both male and female respondents named comedy most often; yet, for women, this was followed by love stories (named by 26 per cent) and musicals (17 per cent), whereas only 2 per cent and 10 per cent of men, respectively, listed these types as their favourites; even worse, 13 per cent of men listed both musicals and love stories among their *least* preferred types of films (Newpaper Advertising Bureau 1974: 7, 61; see results of surveys of teenage girls reported in Anon. 1965b and *Seventeen* 1967). Finally, there was evidence that women selected the film when older couples went to the cinema (Anon. 1974c); hence alienating them also meant that their boyfriends and husbands no longer attended epic romances and musicals either. This undermined the audience base for traditional roadshows, which, as noted earlier, needed to attract an all-inclusive audience to be profitable.

By 1970, the sense that movie theatres were no longer a hospitable place for many segments of the potential audience had become so pronounced that it was a major factor in the reception and success of the two biggest hits of the year. While *Love Story* did by no means receive only positive reviews upon its release in December 1970, the film was widely understood as a successful return to the kind of traditional Hollywood storytelling that, according to critics, had become overshadowed in the late 1960s by thematically and formally challenging films. The *Los Angeles Times* opined:

> Having learned to be brutally candid in word and deed, cynical, pessimistic, unsparing – discoveries which are by no means unimportant – the movies tended to forget that all of us would in fact rather be romantic, idealistic, optimistic, and that if we have a capacity for violence we have a larger capacity for caring ... If you have forgotten you could leave a movie feeling good rather than depressed, you might just want to join the queue outside *Love Story*. (Champlin 1970a)

For *Time* it was the beginning of a 'counter-revolution' against 'sexual license and 'X'-rated sprees' (Kanfer 1970). For the *Saturday Review* the film was a reminder of 'what movies once were all about: ... a catharsis that was all the more joyous because it reaffirmed our essential humanity' (Knight 1971). The magazine concluded that, together with *Airport*, '*Love Story* is going to bring back to the theaters large sections of that "lost audience" that hasn't gone to a movie in years.' (Three years later, similar comments were made about *The Sting*; see for example, Anon. 1973 and Meade 1973.)

When the 'G'-rated *Airport* had received its initial roadshow release in February 1970, *Variety* had described it as 'a handsome, often dramatically involving $10-million epitaph to a bygone brand of filmmaking' (Elley 2000: 11). According to *Entertainment World*, 'it's heartening that Hollywood still occasionally surfaces from the contemporary, psychedelic subculture and produces what should be a whoppingly successful, old-fashioned film' (Gilbert 1970). The *Los Angeles Times* found the film 'breathtaking in its celebration of anything which used to work when Hollywood was younger and we were all more innocent', and found it to be 'a deliberate appeal to the sedentary majority' who had come to prefer watching television to going to the movies (Champlin 1970b). The *Hollywood-Citizen News* pointed out that 'you can take your children along', and also that the film's producer had an excellent track record with Doris Day 'women's pictures', thus suggesting that *Airport* was less male-oriented than most high-profile releases of those years (Scott 1970).

These themes recurred in the reception of subsequent disaster movies. In its review of *The Poseidon Adventure*, for example, the *Los Angeles Herald-Examiner* wrote that the film was 'an old-fashioned adventure

FIGURE 8 *Airport* (George Seaton, 1970)

suspense thriller ... something of an aquatic *Airport*' which departed from Hollywood's recent preoccupations insofar as it made 'no social comment. There's no nudity. No drugs. No homosexuality ... only the man in the street may like *The Poseidon Adventure* – but he and she will like it very much indeed' (Scott 1972). Similarly, the *Evening Outlook* noted under the headline 'At Last – Good Family Film': 'If you have been wondering what happened to old-fashioned movies ... all-star casts, suspense, adventure and something you take the kids to without blushing, the answer is, they are back ... There is no sex, no nudity, no drugs' (Gropenwaldt 1972). While reviewers of disaster movies wrote increasingly – and ever more critically – about costs, special effects and technological spectacle, they explicitly related the films back to the tradition of big-budget epic filmmaking. *Boxoffice* highlighted *Earthquake*'s 'monumental mesh of stunts, effects and editing that harkens back to former Hollywood eras' (Anon. 1974d). The *Hollywood Reporter* described the film as 'one of the biggest entertainments of epic-style filmaking (sic) history' (Anon. 1974e), and also compared *The Towering Inferno* to the epics of Cecil B. DeMille (Dorr 1974).

It would seem, then, that at the same time that the major studios, in the wake of the huge losses of 1969/70, withdrew from the production of traditional roadshow epics and musicals, they invested heavily, and often very successfully, into a new form of big-budget family entertainment, which was modeled on *Airport*. It is important to note that while the budgets for disaster movies (*Airport*, $10m; *The Poseidon Adventure*, $5m; *Earthquake*, $7m; *The Towering Inferno*, $15m; *Airport 1975*, $4m) were clearly above the average cost for a studio release (less than $2m in 1971 and $2.5m in 1974), they were far below the budgets of the most expensive roadshow epics and musicals, which cost in excess of $20m (Finler 2003: 123, 269; Steinberg 1980: 50). Thus, when abandoning the traditional roadshow, the majors shifted most of their biggest investments into what, for a while, was an eminently profitable new form of family entertainment (occasional flops notwithstanding). The high-profile releases and enormous success of these films, especially from 1972 to 1974, in turn appear to have achieved what the reviewers of *Airport* and *Love Story* had been hoping for, namely to bring back to the cinema many of the people who had stopped attending. By 1975, the share of the population aged 18 and over who never went to the cinema had dropped to 40 per cent, as compared to 43 per cent in 1972 (Jowett 1976: 486; Gertner 1979: 32A).

Conclusion

In the late 1960s the major studios invested heavily in two divergent production trends. On the one hand, on the back of the astonishing success
of traditional roadshow epics and musicals in movie theatres in the early
to mid-1960s and their ongoing popularity as evidenced by extended runs,
television ratings and audience polls after 1966, the studios dramatically
increased their output of these kinds of films. On the other hand, they
released a growing number of films – including both relatively cheap productions such as the surprise hit *The Graduate* and big-budget star vehicles
such as *Butch Cassidy and the Sundance Kid* – which broke long-established taboos of filmic representation, especially with respect to sex, violence and race relations. While the taboo-breaking films were particularly
attractive to some audience segments, notably male youth, they alienated
large numbers of Americans (in particular older people and women and
also, possibly, those with little education), many more of whom stopped
going to the movies. By 1970, it was clear that, due to overproduction and
the alienation of key audience segments, the large output of traditional
roadshows could not be maintained. In the wake of massive losses generated by these films in 1969/70, the major studios used *Airport*, a huge hit
in 1970, as the model for a new kind of big-budget family entertainment.
(Interestingly, the other breakaway hit of 1970, *Love Story*, appears to have
been a less successful model for future productions, perhaps because its
attractions were less diverse; in particular, the film did not have much to
offer to children.) With a string of high-profile and very successful disaster
movies, especially *The Poseidon Adventure* and *The Towering Inferno*, as
well as other old-fashioned entertainments (most notably *The Sting*) the
studios did indeed win back some of the previously lost audience after
1972. At the same time, the output and success of films featuring sex,
violence, sacrilege and/or racial conflict continued, particularly with the
superhits *The Godfather*, *The Exorcist*, *Blazing Saddles*, *Jaws*, *One Flew
Over the Cuckoo's Nest* and *Rocky*.

As we have seen, an important precondition for the emergence of such
films had been the weakening and abandonment of the Production Code
from 1966 to 1968. The question remains why the MPAA's attitude towards
the Code had changed in 1966 and why there was such a strong interest in
the breaking of filmic taboos among both filmmakers and some audiences.

FROM THE ROADSHOW ERA TO THE NEW HOLLYWOOD II

In *Time* magazine's exploration of the wider cultural context of the Hollywood renaissance in 1967, artistic developments in European cinema came top of the list. *Time* referenced the French New Wave and a related movement in Czechoslovakia as well as Italian filmmakers Michelangelo Antonioni and Gillo Ponteverco and the Pole Roman Polanski. Indeed, the script for *Bonnie and Clyde* had first been offered to leading French filmmakers Francois Truffaut and Jean-Luc Godard before the American Arthur Penn took over, and the major Hollywood studios were now offering contracts to European directors such as Antonioni and Polanski. Beyond the cinema, there was 'the questioning of moral traditions, the demythologising of ideas, the pulverising of aesthetic principles in abstract painting, atonal music and the experimental novel' (Kanfer 1971: 325). The article also referenced developments in American society at large, for example when explaining that the extreme violence of *Bonnie and Clyde* could be justified as 'a commentary on the mindless daily violence of the American 1960s' (ibid.). Most sensitive to such developments was, according to *Time*, a young generation of filmmakers and executives who fostered innovation within the film industry. These included directors such as Coppola (28 at the time) and Penn (45) as well as top executives like Robert Evans (37), Richard Zanuck (34) and David Picker (36). Some of these had come up through the Hollywood ranks, while others came from the theatre, television or film school.

In the first section of this chapter, I shall trace the liberalisation and polarisation of public opinion in the US across the 1960s and 1970s, which affected the kinds of films which audiences wanted to see and filmmakers wanted to make. The second section profiles the group of executives and filmmakers who came to dominate Hollywood in the late 1960s and early 1970s, outlining their shared background and outlook, as well as the re-organisation of the film industry which facilitated their rise.

The liberalisation and polarisation of public opinion

There is general agreement among historians that the 1960s were a decade of tremendous social change in the US, and that one key aspect of this change was an increasing internal division of American society and a polarisation of the opposing beliefs, attitudes and actions of dif-ferent social groups – black and white, male and female, young and old, liberal and conservative, the 'silent majority' and the 'counterculture' (for a recent study of the 1960s which in turn has an extensive bibliography see Isserman & Kazin 2004). Film historians have offered detailed accounts of how Hollywood films across the 1960s and into the 1970s were affected by such developments in American society (most notably, Ray 1985: chs. 8–10, and Ryan & Kellner 1988: chs. 1–6). Building on their work, I want to concentrate on one particular way of measuring social change, namely opinion polls, and outline changes in certain areas of public opinion which can be seen to underpin the changing outlook of filmmakers, audiences and regulators, and thus the changing hit patterns. In order to illustrate key trends, I make use of some of the raw survey data which the secondary lit-erature on American public opinion usefully reprints (see Ladd & Bowman 1998; Mayer 1993: 343–493; Yankelovich 1974).

In my use of political labels, I draw on William Mayer's characterisa-tion of conservatism, which he sees as being guided by the following principles:

> The belief in a universal, transcendent moral order, supported and sanctioned by organised religion ... A respect for tradition and a consequent distrust of radical innovation ... The crucial importance of private property ... The necessity of social classes and orders, which are both a natural result of basic inequalities in mind, body, and character, and a requisite for civilised society ... Support for free enterprise and a competitive market system ... A distrust of

centralised governmental power ... A conviction that human nature contains an ineradicable element of sin and corruption ... A vehement opposition to communism. (1993: 12–13)

For the sake of simplicity, I use the term 'liberal' to refer to a political outlook that opposes the above principles. Hence much of what happens to public opinion in the 1960s and into the 1970s can be summarised as liberalisation. I start with trends across the general population, which, I assume, broadly affected all filmmakers and all of their potential audiences. I then look more closely at youth, who, as we have seen, due to their increasing number and their traditionally high frequency of cinemagoing can be seen as the engine driving the changes in movie hit patterns.

Let us start with sex. Any consideration of changing attitudes about sex in 1960s and 1970s America needs to acknowledge first of all how surprisingly conservative – by today's standards – those attitudes were, which means that cinematic representations considered perfectly harmless today may have been perceived as genuinely shocking at the time. For example, as late as 1969, 68 per cent of Americans said that 'it is wrong for a man and a woman to have sex relations before marriage'; only 21 per cent felt it was 'not wrong' while the rest were undecided (Mayer 1993: 385). However, the trend was clearly towards more liberal attitudes. By 1973, objections to pre-marital sex had dropped to 48 per cent and acceptance had more than doubled to 43 per cent. Changing attitudes towards the availability of information about birth control indicate that such liberalisation was a longer-term trend. Support for availability grew fairly steadily from 73 per cent in 1959 to 91 per cent in 1974, while objections dropped from 14 per cent to 8 per cent during this period (1993: 388). In particular, there was strong and growing support for providing teenagers with information about sex. In 1970, 65 per cent of respondents approved of sex education in schools, and in 1974 78 per cent were in favour of giving birth control information to teenagers (1993: 389). Increasingly liberal sexual attitudes also had a strong impact on issues of representation. Objections to 'pictures of nudes in magazines' dropped from 75 per cent of respondents in 1969 to 55 per cent in 1973, and to nudes on the Broadway stage from 83 per cent to 65 per cent (1993: 385). The proposition that 'sexual materials provide an outlet for bottled-up impulses' gained support in the early 1970s, rising from 33 per cent in 1970 to 55 per cent in 1973 (1993: 388).

However, objections to certain sexual practices and representations remained undiminished. Throughout the 1970s, about 70 per cent of Americans believed that 'sexual relations with someone *other* than the marriage partner' were 'always' or 'almost always' wrong, as were homosexual relations (Mayer 1993: 386–7). The increasing visibility of hardcore pornography – as, for example, in the two hardcore top-ten movie hits of 1972 and 1973 – seems to have provoked a backlash. The proposition that 'sexual materials lead to breakdown of morals' gained support, rising from 51 per cent in 1975 to 57 per cent in 1978 (1993: 387). Support for 'laws against the distribution of pornography' was very high and still grew slightly from 89 per cent in 1973 to 91 per cent in 1978 (1993: 390). This kind of counter-reaction – insofar as it affected cinema audiences as well as filmmakers and studio executives – may be at the heart of the declining importance of sex in hit movies after 1973. In other words, the backlash against sexual explicitness prevented certain kinds of sexually-themed films from becoming major hits.

When turning to attitudes about race, once again the general conservativism of American public opinion is noteworthy. For example, in 1968 – when *Guess Who's Coming to Dinner* was still in cinemas – 76 per cent of white respondents 'disapprove(d) of marriage between whites and non-whites', and in 1966 43 per cent of whites said they would even object 'if a member of your family wanted to bring a Negro/black friend home to dinner' (Mayer 1993: 368). Despite these widespread racist attitudes, the period saw an increasing acceptance of African-Americans among whites. Disapproval of interracial marriage dropped from 94 per cent in 1958 to 58 per cent in 1978, and of black dinner guests from 45 per cent in 1963 to 27% per cent in 1977. White support for the proposition that 'Negroes/ blacks should have as good a chance as white people to get any kind of job' grew from 48 per cent in 1946 to 83 per cent in 1963 and 96 per cent in 1972 (1993: 366). White acceptance of a potential 'generally well-qualified' black presidential candidate nominated by their own party more than doubled between 1958 (37 per cent said they would vote for such a candidate) and 1978 (76 per cent) (ibid.). On the one hand, these figures confirm the continuing potential for controversy of racial representations, while also suggesting that the increasing acceptance of black film protagonists (presented as scientists, police detectives, firemen and sheriffs as well as maids, criminals and musicians) was in line with changing public opinion.

FIGURE 9 *Guess Who's Coming to Dinner* (Stanley Kramer, 1967)

Similarly, the increasing representation of other racial and ethnic groups, occasionally as protagonists, was in line with a movement towards, and increasing acceptance of, cultural pluralism in 1970s America. In addition to Native American, Asian-American and Hispanic-American self-assertion, 'emulating the rhetoric of black nationalism, many white ethnic groups in the 1970s also began to speak about "community", group "strength", "survival" and "cultural richness"' (Pleck 2000: 63).

Whereas changing attitudes towards sex, race relations and ethnicity ran parallel to changing hit patterns, with regards to gender equality public opinion developed in the opposite direction to successful filmic representations. Over the decades, an increasing share of Americans approved of 'a married woman earning money in business or industry if she has a husband capable of supporting her': 21 per cent in 1938, 55 per cent in 1969 and 70 per cent in 1975 (Mayer 1993: 393). Support for the proposition that 'women should have an equal role with men in running businesses, industry, and government' grew from 46 per cent in 1972 to 57 per cent in 1978, while the share of those who believed that 'women's place is in the home' dropped from 29 per cent to 21 per cent during this period (1993: 395). Furthermore, in the mid-1970s just over 50 per cent of Americans were in favour of the Equal Rights Amendment to the US constitution, and, because many respondents were undecided, outright opposition was a clear minority opinion (1993: 405–6). Willingness to vote for a potential female presidential candidate nominated by one's party increased from 52 per cent in 1955 to 73 per cent in 1975 (1993: 394). Despite the fact that support for gender equality was probably higher among women than among men, these figures indicate that a large and growing number of men must have supported it as well in the late 1960s and 1970s (see the discussion of youth opinion below).

As we have seen, however, breakaway hits from 1967 to 1976 tended to be narrowly focused on male protagonists, marginalising women in the process. A quantitative content analysis of hit movies found that only 26 per cent of all (major and minor) characters during the decade 1966–75 were female, a percentage which had not improved from the preceding decade; what is more, women were less likely to be given positive character ratings, and were more likely to be driven by greed or malevolence than in preceding or subsequent decades (Powers, Rothman & Rothman 1996: 154, 164, 167). It would appear, then, that male filmmakers in their productions, and male cinemagoers in their film selections, went against the trend of increasing support for women's rights. Films seem to have fulfilled a compensatory function here. In the cinema, men could withdraw from social reality, in which they acknowledged the demands that women could legitimately make on them, into a world in which women were quite marginal or altogether absent.

When it comes to interest in foreign affairs, developments in hit movies and in public opinion were in tune with each other. As we have seen, the New Hollywood Top 14 contrasted sharply with the Roadshow Era Top 14 by turning away from foreign settings and concentrating instead on the US itself. A similar shift in focus can be found in many, though by no means all, lesser hits across the 1960s and 1970s. At the same time, public support for the proposition that the US 'should stay out of world affairs' increased from 16 per cent in 1965 to 36 per cent in 1975 (Mayer 1993: 424), and for the proposition that the US 'should mind its own business internationally' from 18 per cent in 1964 to 41 per cent in 1976 (1993: 425). While only a small minority of Americans were in favour of withdrawal from the United

Nations (rising from 5 per cent in 1962 to 16 per cent in 1975), by the late 1960s the majority felt that the UN was not doing a 'good job'; in addition to those who were unsure about the UN's performance (about 15 per cent), those who judged it to do a 'poor job' grew from 26 per cent in 1954 to 51 per cent in 1975 (1993: 430–1). In 1976, only 46 per cent of Americans agreed that the US 'should cooperate fully with the United Nations' (down from 72 per cent in 1964), while 41 per cent disagreed (up from 16 per cent in 1964) (1993: 431).

The increasing demand for withdrawal from international entanglements was connected to the growing perception of the Vietnam War as a foreign policy disaster, and of the Soviet Union as a foreign partner rather than an enemy. The share of Americans who felt that 'the United States made a mistake sending troops to fight in Vietnam' rose from 24 per cent in 1965 to 58 per cent in 1969, and support for the immediate withdrawal of American troops rose from 9 per cent in 1964 to 29 per cent in 1968 and 41 per cent in 1972 (Mayer 1993: 432–3). At the same time, the share of Americans who held 'highly negative' views of the Soviet Union dropped from 78 per cent in 1954 to 48 per cent in 1966 and 21 per cent in 1973 (1993: 408). Belief in the possibility 'to reach a peaceful settlement of differences with Russia' grew from 44 per cent in 1963 to 57 per cent in 1964; with respect to a closely related question about the ability to reach 'long-term agreements to help keep the peace' between the two countries, 69 per cent of respondents gave a positive answer in 1973 (1993: 416–7).

Thus, it is possible to identify a neo-isolationist tendency in American public opinion, which seems to have been mirrored in many of the films that were being made and especially in the films selected (and thus turned into hits) by cinemagoers. It is also worth pointing out, however, that foreign policy issues remained deeply divisive. With respect to the Vietnam War, in 1968 as many Americans labelled themselves 'doves' as those labelling themselves 'hawks' (about 40 per cent each), and in 1970 34 per cent demanded 'complete victory' as compared to 39 per cent demanding immediate withdrawal (1993: 433–4). Furthermore, despite the belief in the possibility of peaceful coexistence with the Soviet Union, in 1973 43 per cent of Americans judged communism as the 'worst' form of government (1993: 410). In the light of such divisions in public opinion, it is perhaps understandable that Hollywood wanted to avoid films taking an explicit stand on Vietnam or US/Soviet relations, because they were likely to alienate a substantial portion of the potential audience. However, the portrayal of military combat in Second World War films and westerns allowed for a more ambiguous, allegorical approach to contemporary foreign policy.

Finally, the turn from foreign to domestic issues in both public opinion and the majority of hit movies was connected to a rapidly intensifying concern about problems in American society. Thus, support for the proposition that 'we shouldn't think so much in international terms but concentrate more on our own national problems and building up our strength and prosperity here at home' grew from 55 per cent in 1964 to 77 per cent in 1974 (Mayer 1993: 426). Americans had growing concerns – caused primarily, it seems, by domestic developments – about 'the future facing you and your family'; in 1965, 71 per cent were 'generally satisfied' with their future, but only 45 per cent in 1971 (Ladd & Bowman 1998: 28). There were specific concerns about a wide range of important institutions and organisations. When asked whether one 'can trust the government in Washington to do what is right', the answer 'just about always' was selected by a decreasing share of respondents: 17 per cent in 1966 and 2 per cent in 1974. A rapidly increasing share chose 'only some of the time': 22 per cent in 1964 and 62 per cent in 1976 (1998: 105). When asked whether 'the people running the government are a little crooked', 24 per cent answered that 'quite a few' were crooked in 1958, while 45 per cent chose this answer in 1974; during the same period, the share of those answering 'hardly any' dropped from 26 per cent to 10 per cent (1998: 82). There was a growing perception that government was 'run by a few big interests looking out for themselves', a proposition supported by 29 per cent of respondents in 1964 and 66 per cent in 1976 (1998: 109).

These big interests included corporations and the military. The share of those who expressed 'a great deal' of confidence in 'big business or major corporations' dropped from 55 per cent in 1966 to 16 per cent in 1974, while those who had 'hardly any' confidence rose from 5 per cent to 33 per cent (Ladd & Bowman 1998: 129). Confidence in the military also collapsed, from 62 per cent answering 'a great deal' in 1966 to 27 per cent in 1971, while the share expressing 'hardly any' confidence rose from 5 per cent to 20 per cent (1998: 122). Organised religion was also affected by this trend: 41 per cent expressed 'a great deal' of confidence in 1966, only 27 per cent in 1971 (1998: 123). Confidence in 'organised labour' was low to begin with, and dropped further, from 22 per cent answering 'a great deal' in 1966 to

10 per cent in 1976 (1998: 128). The early to mid-1970s also saw decreasing levels of confidence in the police and law firms (1998: 136–7). Interestingly, confidence in television news and newspapers decreased from 1966 to 1972, but then rose again, presumably responding to the impact of major news stories, notably the Vietnam War and Watergate (1998: 124–5).

These changing perceptions of major institutions and organisations in American society provide the context for the popularity of what I have called procedurals. These films tend to build precisely on increasing levels of distrust and criticism, while also usually balancing the negative portrayal of one organisation or profession, often represented by corrupt individuals, with the positive representation of another, usually typified by heroic professionals.

It is reasonable to assume that both filmmakers and their audiences were caught up in the above trends in American public opinion, rather than constituting subcultures that resisted those changes. Indeed, there is evidence that the generations of filmmakers who rose to dominance in Hollywood in the late 1960s (those born in the 1920s and 1930s as well as baby boomers) were at the forefront of certain changes in attitudes, beliefs and values in society, acting as a kind of vanguard (more about this below). Correspondingly, many of these changes affected young, educated people, who constituted the majority of the cinema audience, more than other population segments.

This is demonstrated by a series of surveys of 16–25-year-olds, with a particular focus on college students, in the late 1960s and early 1970s. Summarising the findings of these surveys, Daniel Yankelovich notes that in the late 1960s 'a widening "generation gap" appears in values, morals and outlook, dividing young people (especially college youth) from their parents', while a similar gap also occurred 'between college students and the noncollege majority' (1974: 4). These gaps concerned attitudes towards sex and race relations (with students being more liberal than noncollege youth and older people); attitudes about violence (more frequently endorsed by students than by others, if in support of a good cause) and law and order (seen more critically by students than by others); and 'criticisms of major institutions, such as political parties, big business, the military, etc' (with students being the harshest critics) (1974: 4–5). In the early 1970s, some of the student attitudes softened. Violence was increasingly rejected, 'even to achieve worthwhile objectives'; 'students show greater acceptance of law and order requirements'; and criticisms of 'some major institutions are tempered' (ibid.). At the same time, the attitudes of non-college youth and older people changed in the direction of those held by students, as far as sex, race relations and the criticism of major institutions were concerned.

Let us take a look at some figures illustrating these trends. In 1969, only 34 per cent of college students judged 'casual premarital sexual relations' to be wrong, whereas 57 per cent of non-college youth thought so (Yankelovich 1974: 24). Furthermore, as we saw above, 68 per cent of all Americans thought that premarital sex was wrong (without the specification that it was 'casual', which means that even in a committed relationship pre-marital sex was judged to be wrong). By 1973, the figure for noncollege youth had come down to 34 per cent, the same percentage as that for students in 1969, and for the population at large to 48 per cent; at the same time, the figure for students had dropped to 22 per cent (1974: 24, 67). From 1969 to 1973, the share of students who welcomed 'more acceptance of sexual freedom' grew from 43 per cent to 61 per cent, while the figure for noncollege youth was 47 per cent in 1973 (1974: 66, 90). Hence, college students constituted a vanguard for liberal attitudes towards sex, with the rest of the population initially holding much more conservative views, yet moving strongly in a more liberal direction. It is not clear whether the 'backlash' against sexual liberalisation observed in the general population also occurred amongst youth, but it is worth noting that in 1973 'cracking down on pornography in movies, books, etc' was favoured by 26 per cent of students and 44 per cent of non-college youth (as compared to the vast majority of older people) (1974: 124).

While not directly comparable to surveys of the general population cited above, the Yankelovich youth surveys also registered high levels of support for women's rights. For example, in 1973, over 90 per cent of respondents (both students and noncollege youth) believed in 'equal pay ... for equal work' and over 70 per cent in women's right 'to take the initiative in sex relations'; a majority said that the claims 'that a woman's place is in the home' and 'that women are more emotional and less logical than men' were blatantly wrong (Yankelovich 1974: 98). It is important to note that the figures for female respondents were only slightly higher than for male and female respondents combined (1974: 102), which means that male respondents were almost as supportive of women's rights and gender equality as were women. This would seem to support the speculation presented earlier about the compensatory function of cinematic fictions for male viewers.

The youth surveys also registered exceptionally high levels of discontent with American society (once again not directly comparable with the adult surveys cited above but in all likelihood far exceeding the discontent among older people). In 1969, 99 per cent of college students agreed 'strongly or partially' with the proposition that 'business is too concerned with profits and not with public responsibility'; 78 per cent with the proposition that 'basically we are a racist nation'; and 58 per cent with the proposition that 'the establishment unfairly controls every aspect of our lives; we can never be free until we are rid of it' (Yankelovich 1974: 73). By 1973, similar shares of noncollege youth agreed with these propositions, and the majority of both students and, to a lesser extent, noncollege youth felt that many groups were discriminated against in American society, including Native Americans, Hispanics and African-Americans (1974: 122–3). Furthermore, in 1969, 'fundamental reform or elimination' of the following institutions was demanded by large numbers of college youth: political parties (58 per cent), the military (61 per cent), trade unions (43 per cent), and big business (38 per cent, going up to 54 per cent in 1973); the following year, 69 per cent of college youth wanted fundamental reform or elimination of the penal system (1974: 72). Once again, noncollege youth were initially less critical, but became much more so by 1973 (1974: 122).

It would seem that these kinds of attitudes underpinned many of the hits of the late 1960s and early 1970s, and in particular help to explain the popularity of criminal protagonists, who removed themselves from a mainstream life perceived to be determined by big business, corrupt government and 'the establishment'. However, it also has to be noted that, like the American population in general, young people were increasingly concerned about the decline of law and order (Yankelovich 1974: 73, 123–4, 127; Mayer 1993: 263–70, 358–60). Furthermore, we must not forget that most young Americans shared a fundamental belief in the viability of the American system and its ability to overcome any shortcomings. In 1973, 67 per cent of students and 46 per cent of noncollege youth agreed with the following statement: 'There are flaws in our society, but we are flexible enough to solve them'; only 21 per cent and 25 per cent respectively demanded 'radical change' or wholesale replacement of the social system

(Yankelovich 1974: 122). Belief in what Yankelovich called 'traditional American values' (for example profitmaking, commitment to career, private property, self-sufficiency, control of one's destiny and competition) remained high even among students during this period (1974: 68). Thus, if – as commentators at the time pointed out – many films of the late 1960s and 1970s contained a certain degree of cynicism, this did not reflect public opinion, but once again appears to have fulfilled a compensatory function. Whereas social reality was perceived as a realm which demanded the vigorous application of traditional virtues so as to bring about improvements, the cinema could be perceived as an alternative realm where, occasionally, one might indulge in the questioning of all values and of the purpose of all action, even embrace spectacular death instead of a humdrum life. In sharp contrast with this fantasy, procedural films were closely modelled on the basic outlook of Americans during this period, insofar as they pitted heroic professionals against failing institutions and, in most cases, through their victory affirmed the self-healing power of the social system.

In conclusion, then, we can note that across the 1960s (and into the 1970s), Americans, led by youth, developed more liberal attitudes towards sex, although extremely restrictive views also persisted at surprisingly high levels, and against censorship. Americans grew more assertive about their ethnic identities and were increasingly in favour of racial equality, although this remained a divisive issue. Equally divisive were debates about the legitimacy of violence; opposition to the Vietnam war grew across the population, while young people became more supportive of violent protest. Thus, the weakening and replacement of the Production Code was in line with public opinion, and subsequent representations of sex, violence, race and ethnicity in hit movies responded both to their topicality as social issues and to the ongoing liberalisation of attitudes. At the same time, the increasing polarisation of public opinion across the 1960s, especially between young and old, made it ever more difficult for the major studios to hold on to their traditional all-inclusive audience, and encouraged them to pursue those population segments that attended cinemas most frequently (young, educated, middle-class males), even if it meant alienating others, especially where sexual, racial and violent representations were concerned.

Across the years 1967–76, the focus of the majority of breakaway hits and many top ten films on the US, especially on contemporary American society, was in line with neo-isolationist tendencies in public opinion across the population, that is, a turning away from foreign entanglements. At the same time, the American public, and once again especially youth, became ever more critical of American institutions ranging from government to corporations, so that the withdrawal from foreign affairs also served the purpose of offering an in-depth examination of American society itself. This examination proceeded from the basic assumption, shared by almost all Americans, both young and old, that US society, despite all its problems, did not require radical change, but needed gradual improvements, which were well within reach, as was demonstrated in the many procedurals that became hits during this period.

The above analysis relates changing hit patterns to changes in public opinion. However, this is not the whole story. In addition to responding to external developments, Hollywood underwent organisational changes, which offer further explanations for Hollywood's shifting conception of its audience, the removal of the Production Code, the rise of taboo-breaking films and the overall focus of hit movies on contemporary America.

Corporate and generational change in Hollywood

The major studios' structures and hierarchies underwent radical change in the 1950s and 1960s, brought about by the ageing of previously dominant groups and by corporate re-organisations. These re-organisations included the takeover of United Artists by a group of entertainment lawyers in 1951 and its 1967 acquisition by TransAmerica, a financial business branching out into entertainment; the takeover of Universal by Decca, a record company, in 1951, with both in turn being acquired in the early 1960s by MCA, at the time one of the largest entertainment companies in the US, with a particular strength in television production; the 1966 takeover of Paramount by Gulf & Western, a conglomerate active across a range of industries which had begun to invest heavily in the entertainment sector, including publishing, television and music; the 1967 merger of Warner Bros. and Seven Arts, a television company, with the new entity in turn being absorbed into Kinney National Services, another highly diversified conglomerate investing in a range of entertainment companies; the 1969 purchase of MGM by financier Kirk Kerkorian, who proceeded to dismantle the company (Cook 2000: 301–22; see Monaco 1979: 36–7). Thus, only Columbia, Disney and

20th Century Fox were not subject to takeovers during this period, but they themselves had long branched out into other entertainment industries (notably television, music, publishing and, in Disney's case, theme parks), so that by the late 1960s all of the Hollywood majors were closely associated with companies in other entertainment fields (on their music operations see Smith 1998: 32–44). This association provided a strong impetus for innovation in the film industry, because, throughout the 1960s, hit patterns and marketing strategies were changing rapidly in the publishing industry, the record business and television (see the charts in *People* 2000: 154–6, 218–20, 223–4, 300–4; also see Ozersky 2003 and Alvey 2004 on television ratings charts and audiences, and Burns 1983 on changing hit patterns in singles charts). Because best-selling books were often adapted into hit movies which in turn had best-selling soundtracks, and because publishers, record labels, television companies and film studios found themselves under the same corporate roofs, developments in different entertainment fields were mutually reinforcing, and innovations could spread quickly from one medium to the others. The most obvious example is the transformation of the record industry through rock music. Both Elvis Presley and the Beatles, the two biggest rock acts, also appeared in movies, and rock songs became ever more popular on movie soundtracks across the 1950s and 1960s (see Denisoff & Romanowski 1991). Another example is the rise of procedural novels in the best-seller charts of the late 1950s and early 1960s (Long 1985: 102–3), a trend which later gave rise to blockbusting movie procedurals.

At the same time, the corporate restructuring described above disrupted personnel continuities in the film industry, hastening its generational turnover. Many of the founding fathers of the major studios, mostly nineteenth-century immigrants from Central and Eastern Europe, stayed in charge until the 1950s and even the 1960s, before retirement, death or re-organisations removed them from the top (Gabler 1989, Finler 2003: 51-7). The studios' new owners often appointed relatively young top executives, mostly born in the 1920s and 1930s. Charles Bluhdorn, head of Gulf & Western, for example, put former actor Robert Evans (born in 1930) in charge of Paramount. There also was the crucial appointment in 1966 of Jack Valenti (b. 1921), at the time a special assistant to Democratic president Lyndon B. Johnson, as head of the MPAA. Not bound by Hollywood traditions and liberal in outlook, Valenti had no qualms about dismantling the Production Code. Indeed, Valenti was not the only liberal inhabiting a position of great power in Hollywood in the 1960s. Others included Arthur Krim, one of the lawyers who had taken over United Artists in 1951, and Lew Wasserman, the architect of MCA's takeover of Decca/Universal in the early 1960s (see Brownstein 1992: chs. 5–7). Thus, Hollywood was changing from the top down, with long-held traditions being abandoned in a process of general liberalisation.

At the same time, there was a bottom-up process of change insofar as many young filmmakers, mostly from the same age group as the new top executives, were given a chance to make major Hollywood movies in the 1960s. Their entry into the industry was partly made possible by the ageing of those veteran filmmakers whose formative years had been during the studio system of the 1920s, 1930s and 1940s. I will mainly concentrate my analysis here of generational change among filmmakers on directors and some key producers, although a parallel discussion of writers and stars would be of great interest (importantly, many directors also acted as their own producers and had considerable involvement in script development). I have set aside the British directors of the James Bond films, because the franchise was not director-driven.

By 1967, Cecil B. DeMille, who had been born in 1881 and directed two of the Roadshow Era Top 14 (*The Greatest Show on Earth* and *The Ten Commandments*) as well as *Samson and Delilah*, the highest-grossing film of 1949, and Michael Todd, the creative producer behind *Around the World in Eighty Days*, who had been born in 1907, were long dead. George Cukor (b. 1899, director of *My Fair Lady* as well as *Born Yesterday*, 5th/1950), Walter Wanger (b. 1894, producer of *Cleopatra*), William Wyler (b. 1902, director of *Ben-Hur*), Sam Spiegel (b. 1904, producer of *The Bridge on the River Kwai* as well as *Lawrence of Arabia*, 3rd/1962), Henry Koster (b. 1905, director of *The Robe*) and Robert Stevenson (b. 1905, director of *Mary Poppins* as well as *Old Yeller*, 4th/1957, *The Absent-Minded Professor*, 5th/1961 and *Son of Flubber*, 5th/1963) were in their sixties and either retired or entering the final stage of their careers. Only a few years younger were David Lean (b. 1908, director of *The Bridge on the River Kwai* and *Doctor Zhivago* as well as *Lawrence of Arabia*), Joseph L. Mankiewicz (b. 1909, *Cleopatra*) and Robert Wise (b. 1914, *West Side Story* and *The Sound of Music* as well as *The Sand Pebbles*, 4th/1966). Indeed, most of the leading blockbuster directors of the Roadshow Era belonged to this age group, including Henry King (b. 1896, *David and Bathsheba*, 4th/1951 and *The Snows of Kilimanjaro*, 3rd/1952), Henry Hathaway (b. 1898, *How the West Was Won*, 1st/1962), George Stevens (b. 1904, *Shane*, 3rd/1953 and *Giant*, 3rd/1956), Anthony Mann (b. 1906, *The Glenn Miller Story*, 4th/1954 and *El Cid*, 3rd/1961), Billy Wilder (b. 1906, *Some Like It Hot*, 4th/1959 and *Irma la Douce*, 4th/1963), Otto Preminger (b. 1906, *Exodus*, 3rd/1960), Fred Zinneman (b. 1907, *From Here to Eternity*, 2nd/1953, *Oklahoma!*, 5th/1955 and *A Man For All Seasons*, 5th/1966), Joshua Logan (b. 1908, *Sayonara*, 3rd/1957 and *South Pacific*, 1st/1958), Edward Dmytryk (b. 1908, *The Caine Mutiny*, 2nd/1954, *Raintree Country*, 5th/1957 and *The Carpetbaggers*, 4th/1964), Stanley Kramer (b. 1913, *It's a Mad, Mad, Mad, Mad World*, 2nd/1963), Mark Robson (b. 1913, *Peyton Place*, 2nd/1957) and Richard Fleischer (b. 1916, *20,000 Leagues Under the Sea*, 3rd/1954).

Despite their advanced age (by 1976, all of the above were at least in their sixties), several of these directors directed the occasional top-ten hit between 1967 and 1976, including Stanley Kramer (*Guess Who's Coming to Dinner*, 3rd/1967), Mark Robson (*The Valley of the Dolls*, 7th/1967 and *Earthquake*, 4th/1974), William Wyler (*Funny Girl*, 1st/1968), Robert Stevenson (*The Love Bug*, 2nd/1969, *Bedknobs and Broomsticks*, 10th/1971 and *Herbie Rides Again*, 10th/1974), Henry Hathaway (*True Grit*, 8th/1969), Joshua Logan (*Paint Your Wagon*, 7th/1969), David Lean (*Ryan's Daughter*, 7th/1970) and Richard Fleischer (*Tora! Tora! Tora!*, 8th/1970). There were a few other studio-trained directors from the same generation with hits in the annual top ten of the New Hollywood, among them Gene Kelly (b. 1912, *Hello, Dolly!*, 5th/1969), Don Siegel (b. 1912, *Dirty Harry*, 6th/1971) and Robert Aldrich (b. 1918, *The Dirty Dozen*, 6th/1967 and *The Longest Yard*, 8th/1974).

However, the top hitmakers came from the interwar generation, and almost none of them had come up through the Hollywood studio system; instead they had entered filmmaking from other media. Very few of them had a hit movie before the mid-1960s; indeed, most only started making movies then. The main exception was former *Life* photographer Stanley Kubrick (b. 1928, *2001: A Space Odyssey*, 2nd/1968 and *A Clockwork Orange*, 7th/1971) who already had a major hit with *Spartacus* (1st/1960). Blake Edwards (b. 1922) had started out in television, and directed a string of hit comedies from the 1950s onwards (*Operation Petticoat*, 3rd/1959, *The Great Race*, 5th/1965 and *The Return of the Pink Panther*, 6th/1975).

The largest group of hit directors consisted of those who had been born between the early 1920s and the mid-1930s, received their training and first established their reputations in television (be it live drama, series, variety comedy or documentary) and theatre (drama or ballet), started to make movies in the 1960s and had their first big hits after 1965. This group included Franklin Schaffner (b. 1920, *Planet of the Apes*, 7th/1968, *Patton*, 4th/1970 and *Papillon*, 4th/1973); Gene Saks (b. 1921, *The Odd Couple*, 3rd/1967 and *The Cactus Flower*, 9th/1969); George Roy Hill (b. 1922, *Hawaii*, 2nd/1966, *Thoroughly Modern Millie*, 10th/1967, *Butch Cassidy and the Sundance Kid*, 1st/1969 and *The Sting*, 2nd/1973); Arthur Penn (b. 1922, *Bonnie and Clyde*, 5th/1967 and *Little Big Man*, 6th/1970); Arthur Hiller (b. 1923, *Love Story*, 1st/1970 and *Silver Streak*, 4th/1976); Sidney Lumet (b. 1924, *Murder on the Orient Express*, 9th/1974 and *Dog Day Afternoon*, 4th/1975); Robert Altman (b. 1925, *M*A*S*H*, 3rd/1970); Robert Mulligan (b. in 1925, *Summer of '42*, 4th/1971); Sam Peckinpah (b. 1926, *The Getaway*, 8th/1972); Ted Post (b. 1926, *Magnum Force*, 6th/1973); Mel Brooks (b. 1926, *Blazing Saddles*, 2nd/1974 and *Young Frankenstein*, 3rd/1974); Jack Smight (b. 1926, *Airport 1975*, 7th/1974 and *Midway*, 10th/1976); Norman Jewison (b. 1926, *Fiddler on the Roof*, 1st/1971); Herbert Ross (b. 1927, *The Owl and the Pussycat*, 10th/1970 and *Funny Lady*, 8th/1975); Peter Yates (b. 1929, *Bullitt*, 4th/1968); Richard Donner (b. 1930; *The Omen*, 6th/1976); Mike Nichols (b. 1931, *Who's Afraid of Virginia Woolf?*, 3rd/1966, *The Graduate*, 1st/1967, *Catch-22*, 9th/1970 and *Carnal Knowledge*, 8th/1971); Sydney Pollack (b. 1934, *Jeremiah Johnson*, 5th/1972 and *The Way We Were*, 5th/1973); William Friedkin (b. 1935, *The French Connection*, 3rd/1971 and *The Exorcist*, 1st/1973); and Michael Ritchie (b. 1936, *The Bad News Bears*, 7th/1976). Three more hit directors from this age group – Dennis Hopper (b. 1936, *Easy Rider*, 4th/1969), Paul Mazursky (b. 1930, *Bob & Carol & Ted & Alice*, 6th/1969) and Tom Laughlin (b. 1931, *Billy Jack*, 2nd/1971 and *The Trial of Billy Jack*, 5th/1974) – started out as film actors.

We can note, then, that, notwithstanding some continuities, there was a dramatic generational change among Hollywood's hitmakers in the second half of the 1960s and the early 1970s. Most of the older generation – we can call them the studio generation – born between the mid-1890s and the late 1910s, had spent all their working lives being employed by the major Hollywood studios (in some cases, they had been working for their European counterparts in the early stage of their careers). They were used to the restrictions of the Production Code and highly familiar with the kinds of films that had the most prestige and received the biggest budgets in Hollywood, notably epics and musicals. Furthermore, many of them were foreign-born (for example Wyler, Spiegel, Stevenson, Lean and Preminger) or had immigrant parents, which may have contributed to their affinity for European subject matter so important for the hits of the Roadshow Era. While there were, of course, significant differences within this group of filmmakers, by and large they probably shared a basic outlook with the old studio bosses, seeing the entertainment of the largest possible number of people – young and old, male and female, American and foreign – as their main objective, with a particular emphasis on appealing to mature women who were widely understood to be in charge of the cinemagoing of their children and husbands (see Krämer 1999: 13–14). In general, the studio generation can also probably be characterised as conservative (see the political analyses of Hollywood films especially in the 1950s contained in May 2000 and Powers, Rothman & Rothman 1996).

The new generation of filmmakers rising to prominence in the late 1960s and early 1970s (since the majority had started in television, we can call them the television generation) were born between the early 1920s and the mid-1930s and thus, on average, twenty years younger than the studio generation, and also usually much further removed from their immigrant roots. They were better educated than the studio generation; several of them had studied drama, literature or music (but not film) (see Kindem 1994: 1). Many of these directors (most notably those, like Mike Nichols and Arthur Penn, who worked on Broadway in the 1960s) were used to the range of topics and the kinds of language that could be used in the theatre, and not at all accustomed to the restrictions of the Production Code (see Black 1998: 243). By and large, they were more liberal than their prede-cessors, placed a higher value on the realistic depiction of contemporary American society and understood themselves to be social commentators and artists as well as entertainers.

Evidence for the shared outlook of this group of filmmakers can be found in two main sources. Most comprehensive and systematic is Stephen Powers, David J. Rothman and Stanley Rothman's 1982 survey of a random sample of writers, producers and directors of hit movies made between 1965 and 1982, which must have included many of the directors from the television generation (1996: 252–3). The survey concludes that the majority of hitmakers 'are quite liberal and cosmopolitan, apt to criticise traditional institutions such as religion, the police, the military and the government, and they endorse a new sexual morality' (1996: 51). In all these respects, Hollywood hitmakers were found to be far more liberal than almost all other elite groups in American society as well as being more liberal than the American public as a whole (1996: 52–78). The study also suggests that 'many of the filmmakers see their work as a form of education, as well as entertainment, and use the freedom of the poststudio structure of the industry to try to convey strong political or social messages' (1996: 77).

In addition, Gorham Kindem has conducted a series of interviews with Hollywood directors from the interwar generation who had previously worked in live television drama (additional interviews with members of the television generation can be found, for example, in Gelmis 1971, Koszarski 1977 and Crist 1991). He concludes that these filmmakers regard their television work as 'their most satisfying creative experiences', valuing in particular the quality of the scripts they were working with, and the focus of those scripts on 'very personal, human dramas that reflected the postwar American experience' (1994: 2–3). From the vantage point of the 1990s, they saw 'added realism' as their main contribution to Hollywood cinema (1994: 4).

This helps to explain the particular orientation of the hit movies these directors made from 1966 onwards. As one aspect of their commitment to realism, they aimed to broaden the language that could be used in mainstream films (in some cases, for example *Who's Afraid of Virginia Woolf?*, it was transferred directly from the Broadway stage), and the range of sexual and violent incidents that could be shown (mostly derived from contemporary literature rather than the stage). In their attempt to continue the exploration of contemporary American society they had begun on television and in the theatre, they were likely to choose stories set in contemporary America (alternatively, they could treat the American past as an allegory of the present, as Arthur Penn did with *Bonnie and Clyde*). Their highly critical attitude towards major American institutions lent itself to the procedural form, which allowed them to investigate the shortcomings of, for example, the military, the police, big business and so on. Finally, the realistic, politicised and artistic outlook of the television generation may also help to explain the male bias of their films. Unlike the filmmakers of the studio generation, who had seen themselves in the service of the entertainment needs of the mass audience, especially women (and also audiences in important foreign markets), the television generation did not feel bound by the interests and tastes of women (and foreigners). Instead they tended to make films about what they perceived to be most serious and relevant, which for them were, above all else, the experiences of men in contemporary America.

Let us return to *Time* magazine's emphasis on the influence of European art cinema and European directors, and to the so-called film school generation which is so closely associated with the New Hollywood. In addition to the American-born television generation, several European directors, once again mostly born between the early 1920s and the mid-1930s, made hit movies for the major Hollywood studios during the decade 1967–76. They were associated, to varying degrees, with self-consciously artistic movements and 'new waves' in European cinema and included Franco Zeffirelli (b. 1923 in Italy, *Romeo and Juliet*, 5th/1968), Roman Polanski (b. 1933 in Poland, *Rosemary's Baby*, 7th/1968), John Schlesinger (b. 1925 in the UK, *Midnight Cowboy*, 3rd/1969), John Boorman (b. 1933 in the UK, *Deliverance*, 4th/1972), Bernardo Bertolucci (b. 1940 in Italy, *Last Tango in Paris*, 7th/1973) and Milos Forman (b. 1932 in Czechoslovakia, *One Flew Over the Cuckoo's Nest*, 2nd/1975). Through these directors, there is a direct influence of European art cinema on mainstream hits in the US. This influence is also detectable through the film school education that another group of hitmakers received in the US. This group, born between the late 1930s and the late 1940s, entered Hollywood, mostly via exploitation filmmaking or television, in the late 1960s and early 1970s, and included Francis Ford Coppola (b. 1939, UCLA, *The Godfather*, 1st/1972 and *The Godfather, Part II*, 6th/1974); Sidney J. Furie (b. 1933, Carnegie Institute of Technology, *Lady Sings the Blues*, 10th/1972); George Lucas (b. 1945, University of Southern California, *American Graffiti*, 3rd/1973); and Steven Spielberg (b. 1947, California State College at Long Beach, *Jaws*, 1st/1975).

Closely associated with this group is Peter Bogdanovich, who was born in 1940 and started out as a film critic and documentary filmmaker, before making Hollywood movies, including *The Last Picture Show* (9th/1971), *What's Up, Doc?* (3rd/1972) and *Paper Moon* (8th/1973). Even if Bogdanovich and some film school-trained writers like John Milius (who was born in 1944 and co-wrote *Jeremiah Johnson*, 5th/1972) are included, the impact of the film school generation on the hit lists of 1967–76 pales in comparison with the dominant television generation (film school graduates would only dominate the charts after 1976). A careful examination of formal and stylistic innovation in hit movies would no doubt be able to identify certain characteristics of European art cinema in the work of a wide range of directors (see Krämer 1998a: 306–7). Yet, all things considered, this influence appears to be much less important for the New Hollywood than the model of post-war American theatre and live television drama.

Conclusion

In the late 1960s and early 1970s, Hollywood responded to changes in American public opinion by abandoning the Production Code and producing more and more films which were, broadly speaking, in line with the changing values and concerns of the large number of baby boomers, who were entering their prime cinemagoing age (15–25) during this period. The films that attracted the largest audiences mirrored increasingly liberal attitudes towards sex, race and ethnicity as well as a widespread fascination with, and anxieties about, violence, while inverting the growing egalitarian attitudes towards gender. They also mirrored the neo-isolationist withdrawal from foreign entanglements in public opinion, and an increasingly critical, but fundamentally positive attitude towards the most important institutions of American society. Because public opinion was increasingly polarised, the pursuit of the comparatively liberal youth audience by necessity involved the risk of alienating more conservative older population segments. When these segments stopped going to the cinema, their absence in turn heightened the importance of young cinemagoers for the studios. Studio executives were willing to take this risk and narrow their focus in this way because the youth audience was so numerous and so dedicated to cinemagoing that it constituted a large enough market for Hollywood's operations.

Additionally, the drastic restructuring of the major studios in the 1960s disrupted their traditional ways of doing business and encouraged innovation. Corporate takeovers and diversification brought the studios close to other sectors of the entertainment industry, where changing hit patterns and marketing strategies were observable just as much as, and in important cases earlier than, they were in the film industry. Furthermore, such corporate restructuring removed most of the vestiges of the reign of Hollywood's founding fathers and installed many younger executives, mostly born in the 1920s and 1930s, at the top. This in turn facilitated both the dismantling of the Production Code and the employment of new generations of filmmakers. Most notably, these included a group of largely liberal, socially committed and to some extent self-consciously artistic directors, who also had been born in the 1920s and 1930s, and who had received their training and established their initial reputation in television and theatre rather than the old studio system. When they entered the film industry, mostly from the mid-1960s onwards, they were in a particularly good position to exploit the new freedoms offered by the dismantling of the Production Code. Not least because their outlook was broadly in line with important trends in public opinion among youth, their films soon began to rule the box office charts.

CONCLUSION: 1977 AND BEYOND

On 25 May 1977 the film industry's leading trade paper, *Variety*, published an enthusiastic review of George Lucas' *Star Wars* (reprinted in Salewicz 1998: 123–5), declaring it to be 'a magnificent film', which 'like a breath of fresh air ... sweeps away the cynicism that has in recent years obscured the concepts of valour, dedication and honour'. According to *Variety*, the film drew on, and revived, older forms of Hollywood entertainment, including Flash Gordon serials, Errol Flynn adventures and 'the genius of Walt Disney' (who had died in December 1966, almost exactly a year before *Time* announced the Hollywood Renaissance). Like this older Hollywood, *Star Wars* had 'all-age appeal' and was an 'affirmation of what only Hollywood can put on a screen' – exciting action, spectacular technology and a 'rousing score' combined with sympathetic characters and 'human drama' set in an 'intriguing intergalactic world': 'This is the kind of film in which an audience, first entertained, can later walk out feeling good all over.' In effect, this review declared *Star Wars* to be a repudiation of many of the dominant trends of the New Hollywood (a claim which, as we have seen, had previously been made for disaster movies).

As it turned out, *Star Wars* did not only become the second-biggest hit of all time up to this point (topped only by *Gone With the Wind*, with its numerous re-releases, in the inflation-adjusted all-time chart; see Steinberg 1980: 3), but it also quickly established itself as the key reference point for debates among critics as well as filmmakers and cinemagoers about the pleasures and meanings, the potential and limitations of contemporary Hollywood cinema. Already in November 1977, for example, the *Variety*

FIGURE 10 *Star Wars* (George Lucas, 1977)

review of Steven Spielberg's science fiction film *Close Encounters of the Third Kind* (reprinted in Perry 1998: 108–9) noted: '[The film's] dénouement is light years ahead of the climactic nonsense of Stanley Kubrick's *2001: A Space Odyssey*. Yet, in terms of real empathy with enduring human nature as it is (warts and all), *Close Encounters* lacks the warmth and humanity of George Lucas' *Star Wars*.' Where *2001: A Space Odyssey*, with its abstraction and ambiguity, had once been the benchmark for science fiction films, now it was the 'warmth and humanity' of *Star Wars*.

Film scholars soon responded to this shift, which applied not only to science fiction films, but seemed to affect Hollywood as a whole. By redefining the meaning of the term 'New Hollywood' (now referring to the period since the mid-1970s) or by introducing the notion of a 'New New Hollywood' or of a 'post-modern' American cinema, scholars identified the second half of the 1970s as another period of fundamental change in American film history (see Krämer 1998a: 301–5; for a recent contribution to this debate, see Shone 2004). Once again, broad critical agreements – now on the whole just as negative in their judgements as those about the Hollywood Renaissance had been positive – emerged swiftly. It was said that Hollywood was focusing ever more narrowly on blockbuster productions to be marketed in conjunction with countless tie-in products, and that filmic characterisation and storytelling were undermined by the prominence of merchandising and the films' increasing emphasis on special effects and spectacle (although some dissenters argued that Hollywood had in fact entered a 'neo-classical' period of ever more efficient and effective storytelling). Furthermore, both aesthetically and politically Hollywood was deemed to have become much more conservative. At the heart of this re-orientation of American film culture were, it was widely agreed, science fiction and action-adventure films, most notably those directed and/or produced by George Lucas and Steven Spielberg.

While I would take issue with the negative critical evaluation of Hollywood's big hits since the late 1970s in terms of both their aesthetics and their politics (see Krämer 1998a: 306–7 and 1998b, Thompson 1999, and Powers, Rothman & Rothman 1996), there is no doubt that patterns of success have indeed changed significantly, with 1977 standing out as another major historical turning point. To demonstrate this, I want to compare the biggest hits of the decade from 1977 onwards with the New Hollywood Top 14 of the decade before 1977. Using the inflation-adjusted all-time chart which forms the basis for appendices 2 and 4, I have selected all films from 1977–86 which outdo *One Flew Over the Cuckoo's Nest*, the lowest-ranked film from the New Hollywood Top 14 (the Roadshow Era Top 14 are also all ranked above *One Flew Over the Cuckoo's Nest*). This once again creates a list of fourteen films (see appendix 5; figures for rentals below are taken from Cohn 1993, and those for box office gross from *Variety* 2000: 62–7; in the case of the *Star Wars* films and *Grease*, box office figures were adjusted so as to exclude re-releases after 1986):

1977   *Star Wars* (with rentals of $194m and a box office gross of $323m), *Close Encounters of the Third Kind* ($83m/$156m), *Smokey and the Bandit* ($59m/$127m)

1978   *Grease* ($96m/$153m), *National Lampoon's Animal House* ($71m/$142m), *Superman* ($83m/$134m)

1980   *The Empire Strikes Back* ($142m/$223m)

1981   *Raiders of the Lost Ark* ($116m/$242m)

1982   *E.T. The Extra-Terrestrial* ($229m/$400m), *Tootsie* ($95m/$177m)

1983   *Return of the Jedi* ($169m/$263m)

1984   *Ghostbusters* ($133m/$239m), *Beverly Hills Cop* ($108m/$235m)

1985   *Back to the Future* ($105m/$208m)

Let us first of all examine whether these films have the same exalted status in American film culture from the late 1970s to the mid-1980s as the New Hollywood Top 14 (and the Roadshow Era Top 14) had in their time. The commercial success of *Star Wars* was certainly astonishing. The film's box office total of $323m was equivalent to 14 per cent of all income generated from cinema ticket sales in the US in 1977 ($2,376m), the year when *Star Wars* made most of its money (Finler 2003: 377). This is comparable to the 12 per cent market share of *Jaws*, the record holder among the New Hollywood Top 14, and the 17 per cent share of *The Sound of Music*, the record holder among the Roadshow Era Top 14. The average ticket price in 1977 was $2.23 (2003: 379), which means that 145m tickets were sold for *Star Wars*. This is equivalent to about 65 per cent of the American population in 1977 (however, it is certainly not the case that two-thirds of all Americans actually saw the film in the cinema at the time because there were many repeat viewers; see Earnest 1985: 16). Once again, this percentage is comparable to that for *Jaws* (60 per cent) and *The Sound of Music* (55 per cent).

The impact of *Star Wars* on subsequent film production and audience choices was enormous, most directly through its sequels. Sequels and film series were by no means a new phenomenon. Feature films which continued the story told in a previous film, or which used the same set of characters as an earlier film without establishing any clear chronological sequence or causal connection between events in both films, had been around for a long time (see Simonet 1987). While sequels and series had usually been associated with the low-budget sector, both the Roadshow Era and the New Hollywood saw several highly successful big-budget sequels and series. *Jolson Sings Again* (the third-highest-grossing movie of 1949), for example, was a sequel to *The Jolson Story* (1946), and *Cinerama Holiday* (1st/1955) can be regarded as a sequel to *This is Cinerama* (1st/1952). The biggest success story prior to the *Star Wars* trilogy was the James Bond series, which included *Goldfinger* (3rd/1964), *From Russia With Love* (5th/1964), *Thunderball* (3rd/1965), *You Only Live Twice* (8th/1967), *Diamonds Are Forever* (5th/1971) and *Live and Let Die* (9th/1973) (see appendices 1 and 3). Hit movies with top-ten sequels during the New Hollywood era include: *Funny Girl* (1st/1968) and *Funny Lady* (8th/1975); *The Love Bug* (2nd/1969) and *Herbie Rides Again* (10th/1974); *Billy Jack* (2nd/1971) and *The Trial of Billy Jack* (5th/1974); *The Godfather* (1st/1972) and *The Godfather, Part II* (6th/1974); *Dirty Harry* (6th/1971), *Magnum Force* (6th/1973) and *The*

Enforcer (8th/1976); one might also include *Airport* (2nd/1970) and *Airport 1975* (7th/1974) although hardly any characters are carried over from the first to the second film. *Jaws* also had two sequels, the first of which was a top ten hit in 1978 (top ten hits of the late 1970s are listed in Cook 2000: 501–2).

Thus, the success of the *Star Wars* sequels was not without precedent. However, even the two breakaway hits that the Bond series generated in the mid-1960s pale in comparison with the box office dominance of the *Star Wars* trilogy in the late 1970s and early 1980s. Furthermore, several other breakaway hits of 1977–86 also generated top-grossing sequels, including *Smokey and the Bandit II* (7th/1980), *Superman II* (3rd/1981) and *Indiana Jones and the Temple of Doom* (3rd/1984) (Anon. 1991b: 81–2). The next tier of hit movies below the Top 14 also generated numerous top ten sequels, ranging from *Staying Alive* (9th/1983), the follow-up to *Saturday Night Fever* (3rd/1977), to several sequels of *Star Trek: The Motion Picture* (2nd/1979). Furthermore, several top ten hits from 1977–86 were themselves sequels of pre-1977 top ten hits, including more Bond films and several sequels to *Rocky*. Compared to the decade before 1977, then, sequelisation became a much more important phenomenon in the annual top ten from 1977 onwards, and it was also more blatant, due to the widespread use of numerals in film titles.

The greater prominence of sequels did not, however, affect the market share of the Top 14. Indeed, the market share of the breakaway hits from 1977 to 1986 is comparable to that of the breakaway hits of the New Hollywood and the Roadshow Era. If we add up the grosses for the ten most successful films of the decade 1977–86 (one per year), the total amounts to $2,466m, which is 8 per cent of the total box office earnings in the US during these years (Finler 2003: 377). As we saw in chapter one, the ten highest-grossing films for 1967–76 had a market share of 10 per cent, and the fourteen highest-grossing films for the fourteen years from 1952 to 1965 had a market share of 6 per cent. This means that, contrary to received opinion, the concentration of box office revenues on breakaway hits is slightly *less* pronounced in the decade from 1977 onwards than during the decade before 1977 (but more pronounced than during the Roadshow Era).

Another change concerns the status of film showings on television. As we have seen, until the late 1970s traditional roadshow epics and musicals together with New Hollywood superhits dominated the all-time ratings charts for movies (with only very few made-for-TV movies being able to compete). Indeed, these film broadcasts were among the highest rated programmes of any kind in American television history up to that point. The superhits since 1977 have been unable to match the ratings of earlier hits, and they have also been left far behind by made-for-TV movies and mini-series, season finales of popular series and sports broadcasts since 1977 (*People* 2000: 162). What is more, from the late 1970s onwards, fewer movie nights than before were included in the annual listings of the twenty top-rated TV programmes (*People* 2000: 156–8).

At the same time, however, the superhits of 1977–86 played an important role in the growth, in the late 1970s, of two new delivery systems for audiovisual entertainment, namely cable television and home video. Movies in general, and breakaway hits in particular, were the main attraction of successful pay-cable services such as HBO (see Hilmes 1990) and by the early 1980s they also dominated the sales and rentals of pre-recorded videotapes (see Wasser 2001). The top ten of *Billboard* magazine's first video sales chart, in 1980, include *Superman* and *Grease* (as well as *Saturday Night Fever*); *Superman* is also in the top ten for 1981 (*People* 2000: 110). *Billboard*'s first video rentals chart, in 1982, has *Star Wars* at no. 4; the film also is at no. 8 in the sales chart for the following year, and its first sequel is ranked 8th in the rentals chart for 1985. In 1984, *Raiders of the Lost Ark* is at no. 2 in the sales chart (dropping to no. 7 in 1985) and at the top of the rentals chart. In 1986, *Beverly Hills Cop* is at no. 4 in the sales chart and at no. 2 in the rentals chart (with *Ghostbusters* at no. 5). *E.T.* became one of the all-time best-selling videos after it was finally released in 1989 (see Jamgocyan 1998). Thus, while the Top 14 of 1977–86 no longer dominated the TV ratings charts, they did extremely well on video. Between video sales and rentals, showings on pay-cable and network broadcasts, they continued to reach large segments of the American population at home (as did the superhits of earlier eras; the popularity of films like *The Godfather*, *The Sound of Music* and *Gone With the Wind* on video throughout the 1980s is particularly striking).

The resonance of the Top 14 of 1977–86 across other media is comparable to the resonance breakaway hits had in earlier periods, although the focus shifted to different product categories. The traditional association of superhits with best-selling books and soundtracks as well as Broadway shows is still in evidence in some cases, but it is, in fact, much reduced by comparison with the superhits of preceding eras. The soundtrack for *Grease*, which was based on one of the longest-running shows in Broadway history, was the second best-selling album of 1978, outsold only by the *Saturday Night Fever* soundtrack; both records were among the top-selling albums of all time (*People* 2000: 221–8, 327). The *Beverly Hills Cop* soundtrack was the seventh-biggest-selling album of 1985 and 'Ghostbusters' the ninth-biggest-selling single of 1984. The *E.T. The Extra-Terrestrial Storybook* was the top-selling fiction hardcover of 1983, and the *Return of the Jedi Storybook* took the no. 1 spot in 1982 (2000: 304–5). While many of the other films in the Top 14 – and indeed across the annual top ten – were tied in with novels, soundtracks or singles, by and large these were *less* prominent in the respective charts than the books and records associated with the hits of earlier periods had been (see *People* 2000: 218–25, 298–306).

However, whereas almost all Roadshow Era superhits and most New Hollywood superhits had been based on pre-existing stories in other media, this no longer applied to the superhits of 1977–86. The only films in the Top 14 adapted from a specific non-filmic source were *Grease* and *Superman*, and the two best-selling tie-in novels were based on films rather than the films being based on them. What is more, there were countless other products derived from the films, ranging from t-shirts to toys. While this was by no means unprecedented (Disney films and *Jaws* being important precursors), the amount of merchandise sold on the back of superhits – and also, of course, of lesser hits – increased dramatically (see for example, Prince 2000b: 137–40; for the impact of *Star Wars* and other movie merchandise on the toy industry, see Cross 1997: 202–5). Once again this merchandise in turn helped to promote the films.

What about the status of breakaway hits among audiences, critics and filmmakers? In the light of later critical attacks on the film, it is somewhat surprising to see that, in the late 1970s, *Star Wars* received widespread recognition comparable to the recognition received by *The Graduate* and the rest of the New Hollywood Top 14. *Star Wars* made it onto the annual 'Ten Best' lists compiled by *Time* and the *New York Times* (as did *Close Encounters of the Third Kind*), and was voted the best film of 1977 by the Los Angeles Film Critics Association (Steinberg 1980: 175, 179, 308). The National Board of Review selected *Star Wars* (as well as *Close Encounters of the Third Kind*) as one of the five best English-language films of the year

(1980: 284). Furthermore, *Star Wars* won seven Academy Awards from ten nominations; however, while nominated for Best Picture and Screenplay, it only received Oscars in the technical and crafts categories (the results for *Close Encounters of the Third Kind* were similar) (Elley 2000: 162, 809). Nevertheless, *Star Wars* was immediately recognised as one of the all-time greats. Already in 1977, it was voted one of the ten best American films of all time by members of the American Film Institute, and as one of the ten all-time favourites by readers of the *Los Angeles Times* (2000: 144, 189). The following year, a survey among leading critics conducted by the film magazine *Take One* identified *Star Wars* (and also *Close Encounters of the Third Kind*) as one of the forty best films of the decade 1968–77, and a survey of college students found that *Star Wars* was their second favourite film of all time (after *Gone With the Wind*) (2000: 155–7, 182–3). At the end of the decade *Time* selected *Star Wars* as one of the ten best American films of the 1970s (2000: 179).

Despite all these accolades for *Star Wars*, already in 1977 there were clear signs that the critical status of breakaway hits was changing. As we have seen, *Close Encounters of the Third Kind* was well-received, but much less so than *Star Wars*, and the third breakaway hit of the year, the Burt Reynolds action-comedy *Smokey and the Bandit*, was nowhere to be found on 'Ten Best' lists or at award ceremonies. The film receiving the highest accolades both from critics and the film industry itself was Woody Allen's *Annie Hall*, which was only a minor hit in 1977. In the following decade, Hollywood's breakaway hits were rarely the favourites of critics and industry personnel, although several of them joined the all-time ranks of audience favourites (the Internet Movie Database users chart – as accessed on 14 September 2004 – has *Star Wars* at no. 10, *The Empire Strikes Back* at no. 13 and *Raiders of the Lost Ark* at no. 17; http://www.imdb.com/chart/top). None of the Top 14 of 1977–86 won any of the major Academy Awards (Best Picture, Director, Actor, Actress, Screenplay), which instead went to the next tier of big hits such as *Kramer vs. Kramer* (1st/1979), *On Golden Pond* (2nd/1981), *Terms of Endearment* (2nd/1983), *Out of Africa* (5th/1985) and *Platoon* (3rd/1986), or to films which never even made the annual top ten such as *Coming Home* (1978), *Gandhi* (1982) and *Amadeus* (1984) (see Cook 2000: 501–2; Anon. 1991b: 81–4).

In what ways did the kinds of films which became breakaway hits differ from the New Hollywood Top 14? The first thing to note is that science fiction (the *Star Wars* trilogy, *E.T.*, *Back to the Future*, *Close Encounters of the Third Kind* and *Superman*) and what one might call fantastic comedy-adventures (*Raiders of the Lost Ark* and *Ghostbusters*) clearly dominate the Top 14 of 1977–86, making up nine out of fourteen films, including the top five (see appendix 5). This constitutes a major shift in hit patterns, and this shift is indeed very closely associated with two filmmakers; as directors, writers and/or producers George Lucas and Steven Spielberg were involved with seven of these nine science fiction/fantasy-adventure films, once again including the top five. The New Hollywood Top 14 (as well as the Roadshow Era Top 14) did not include a single science fiction film or fantastic comedy-adventure, nor can many films of these types be found in the annual top ten for 1967–76; the exceptions are *2001: A Space Odyssey* and *Planet of the Apes* in 1968 and *A Clockwork Orange* in 1971, although it also has to be noted that Bond films often featured futuristic technology (see appendix 1).

In addition to constituting a major generic shift in hit patterns, the prominence of science fiction and fantastic comedy-adventures among the breakaway hits from 1977 to 1986 also is reminiscent of (but not quite as complete as) the dominance of three types of films (historical epics, international adventures and musicals) among the Roadshow Era Top 14. What is more, like those earlier breakaway hits, they are family-friendly and addressed to an all-inclusive audience, which is indicated by their 'PG' ratings, by the absence of sex, bad language and graphic violence (unless it is rendered comically), and the playing down of other potentially controversial elements. Indeed, these films actively court children and their parents – in addition to the core audience of teenagers and young adults – insofar as most of them feature young children, teenagers or somewhat child-like adults in stories about familial or quasi-familial relationships; the films also appeal to adults' nostalgic fondness for entertainment forms (such as comic strips, movie serials, fairytales and ghost stories) which they remember from their own childhood (see Krämer 1998b). As is indicated by reviews in *Variety* and a wide range of other newspapers and magazines, these films were certainly perceived at the time as a return to old-fashioned family entertainment (see Krämer 2002b: 186–7, and 2004: 365–6; across the Top 14, we find only two 'R' rated films: *Animal House* and *Beverly Hills Cop*).

It is also possible to detect in these films a return to the epic form (that is the spectacular engagement with key moments in human history) and to spiritual matters, albeit now in the guise of science fiction and fantasy. Following on in many ways from *2001: A Space Odyssey*, the *Star Wars* trilogy is clearly epic and also explicitly spiritual (with its emphasis on 'the Force'). Both *Close Encounters of the Third Kind* and *E.T.* depict a transformative moment in history, namely the encounter with extraterrestrials, and they do so with distinctly religious overtones. *Raiders of the Lost Ark* tells its adventure story, which culminates with a display of divine power, against the backdrop of the rise of fascism. Superman is a kind of saviour figure, and *Ghostbusters* stages a near-apocalypse brought about by an evil supernatural force. No doubt influenced by the success of the above films, especially *Star Wars* and *Close Encounters of the Third Kind*, many more science fiction and fantasy films (as well as some horror movies) with epic and/or spiritual resonances can be found among the annual top ten from 1977 to 1986. They range from *Star Trek – The Motion Picture* (2nd/1979) to *Wargames* (5th/1983), *Cocoon* (6th/1985) and *Aliens* (7th/1986); from *Time Bandits* (9th/1981) and *Heaven Can Wait* (6th/1978) to *Indiana Jones and the Temple of Doom* (3rd/1984) and *The Golden Child* (8th/1986); from *The Amityville Horror* (8th/1979) to *Poltergeist* (7th/1982). Outside science fiction, fantasy and horror, the annual top ten included several 'straight' epics such as the war films *A Bridge Too Far* (10th/1977), *The Deer Hunter* (9th/1978), *Apocalypse Now* (6th/1979) and *Platoon* (3rd/1983), and the female-centered sentimental historical dramas *Out of Africa* (5th/1985) and *The Color Purple* (4th/1985), as well as more films with explicitly religious or spiritual themes such as *Oh, God!* (6th/1977) and *The Karate Kid* (5th/1984). Indeed, the share of hit movies featuring some form of supernatural event increased from 6 per cent in the decade 1966–75 to 26 per cent for 1976–90 (Powers, Rothman & Rothman 1996: 131).

In addition to this renewed emphasis on spirituality and the epic, the Top 14 of 1977–86 also indicate a more prominent role for musicals with pop, rock and country music replacing traditional showtunes (a trend which started in the mid-1970s, as we saw in chapter two). The breakaway success of *Grease* is complemented by other musicals in the annual top ten, including *Saturday Night Fever* (3rd/1977), *Popeye* (10th/1980), *The Blues Brothers* (8th/1980), *Coal Miner's Daughter* (5th/1980), *Annie* (10th/1982), *Best Little Whorehouse in Texas* (9th/1982), *Staying Alive* (9th/1983), *Flashdance* (3rd/1983) and *Footloose* (7th/1984). Another echo of the Roadshow Era Top 14 is the preponderance of calculated blockbusters, that is, films which due to their stars, budget or source material could be expected to do well, the most clear-cut cases being sequels to breakaway hits. As far as budgets are concerned, nine of the Top 14 of 1977–86 were clearly above average, four were just above (*Grease* and *Beverly Hills Cop*) or just below (*Smokey and the Bandit* and *E.T.*), and only *Animal House* was a low-budget film, costing $2.7m at a time when the average budget was $5m (Finler 2003: 42, 95, 123, 190, 269, 298). Since *Animal House* and *E.T.* also lacked established movie stars and were not based on popular source material, they can be seen as the only true surprise hits among the Top 14 – whereas the New Hollywood Top 14 included four big surprises. In many respects, then, the Top 14 and, more generally, the annual top ten of 1977–86, turned away from the most important trends of the New Hollywood and towards older traditions of the Roadshow Era.

At the same time, there are clear continuities with the New Hollywood Top 14. Indeed some trends become more pronounced. Except for the alternative universe of the *Star Wars* films and the 1930s international settings of *Raiders of the Lost Ark*, the films' stories all take place in postwar America, and with the exception of *Grease*, *Animal House* and parts of *Back to the Future* and *Superman*, they are basically set at the time when they were released. The central protagonists of all the films are male (only in *Grease* is the male protagonist complemented by a woman receiving equal attention), and the only woman who gets top billing is Dee Wallace, who plays the mother in *E.T.* As in the preceding decade, the breakaway hits of 1977–86 continue to address social divisions of various kinds, including class differences (most notably in *Animal House*, *Grease* and *Beverly Hills Cop*) and generational tensions (notably through father/son relationships as in the *Star Wars* trilogy and *Back to the Future*).

Arguably, the emphasis on conflictual gender relations and romance is more pronounced than in the New Hollywood Top 14, especially in *Grease* and *Tootsie*, but also in *Smokey and the Bandit*, *Superman* and *Back to the Future*; even the *Star Wars* trilogy, *Raiders of the Lost Ark* and *Ghostbusters* have important screwball-type romantic storylines. More generally, one might characterise the Top 14 of 1977–86, despite the prominence of science fiction, action-adventure and male protagonists, as more female-friendly than the New Hollywood Top 14, due to their avoidance of extreme violence and graphic sex (*Animal House* being an exception), and their frequent emphasis on romantic love and familial relations. Broadening the perspective to include the annual top ten hits and the main Oscar winners certainly confirms this sense that from 1977 onwards Hollywood's commercially and critically most successful films belonged far more often than during the preceding decade to those genres typically preferred by women, that is, musicals, romantic comedies, costume films, contemporary dramas and weepies (Krämer 1999: 99). Furthermore, after a decade in which Quigley's annual lists of top box office attractions had usually included only one woman (mostly Barbra Streisand), from 1977 to 1982, there were on average three (from 1983 the figure went down again) (Moser 1997: 19A).

Another shift concerns the focus on ethnicity in the New Hollywood Top 14 which was largely replaced in the superhits of 1977–86 by an emphasis on racial difference, mostly expressed in a fantastic fashion (through extra-terrestrial/non-human characters in the *Star Wars* trilogy, *Close Encounters*, *Superman*, *E.T.* and *Ghostbusters*) and only once in terms of contemporary social reality (the African-American cop in an all-white setting in *Beverly Hills Cop*). However, several hits (co-)starring African-American stars can be found in the annual top ten, including *Stir Crazy* (3rd/1980), *48 Hours* (8th/1982), *Trading Places* (4th/1983), *The Color Purple* (4th/1985) and *The Golden Child* (8th/1986). After a twelve-year absence from Quigley's top ten box office attractions, African-American stars finally returned from 1982 onwards; Richard Pryor in 1982 was followed by Eddie Murphy from 1983 to 1986, Prince in 1984 and Whoopi Goldberg in 1986 (Moser 1997: 19A). Furthermore, black musicians are featured attractions in *The Blues Brothers* (8th/1980), and there are prominent supporting roles for African-American performers in, for example, the *Rocky* sequels and *An Officer and a Gentleman* (3rd/1982). Indeed, African-Americans made up almost 10 per cent of all (major and minor) characters in hit movies, which is close to their share of the American population (12 per cent) (Powers, Rothman & Rothman 1996: 175–6).

As in previous decades, then, American cinema of the years 1977–86 was dominated by a small group of films, which generated a significant portion of overall film industry income (somewhat smaller, though, than during the New Hollywood), were seen by up to half of the American population in movie theatres (and also on television and video), had a mutually beneficial link to popular tie-in products (with toys now figuring more prominently than books and soundtracks) and exerted a strong influence on future film production and hit patterns (especially through sequels), while also often becoming all-time audience favourites. Unlike in previous decades, however, these breakaway hits were (with one exception) no longer received with widespread acclaim by critics and industry personnel. While their critical standing was thus much reduced, their status as popular-cultural trendsetters had increased, because, rather than adapting stories from other media, they now typically became the sources for such adaptations.

As a group, the fourteen biggest hits of 1977–86 compared in complex ways to the Top 14s of the New Hollywood and the Roadshow Era. Due to the prominence of science fiction and fantastic comedy-adventures (mostly made by Lucas and Spielberg), they were generically less diverse than the New Hollywood Top 14 but more so than the Roadshow Era Top 14. Quite unlike the superhits of the Roadshow Era, they favoured contemporary American settings as much as the New Hollywood Top 14 and, like them, often explored social divisions and foregrounded the actions and experiences of male protagonists. Yet, the Top 14 of 1977–86 were more likely to deal with racial than with ethnic differences and foregrounded gender relations more than the New Hollywood Top 14 had done. They also included fewer surprise hits. Furthermore, they signalled a major revival of the two dominant film types of the Roadshow Era: the musical and the epic. The former, however, now featured rock and pop music, and the latter dealt primarily with fantasy versions of history. At the same time, the Top 14 of 1977–86 moved spirituality and religion back to the centre of American film culture, albeit in the guise of fantasy and science fiction. Perhaps most importantly, building on the success of the disaster cycle, the majority of the Top 14 of 1977–86 revived the Roadshow Era ideal of all-inclusive family entertainment, bringing together youth and children as well as their parents, both male and female, and often doing so by putting familial relationships at the centre of their stories.

There is evidence that the all-inclusiveness of most superhits was connected to a new inclusiveness of the cinemagoing public. As we saw in chapter two, in 1972 the share of people who attended cinemas only infrequently (one or twice a year) or never was 61 per cent among women over 17 and 79 per cent among those who had not completed high school (Jowett 1976: 485–6). By 1983, these figures had come down to 53 per cent for women over 17 and 68 per cent for those without a high school diploma (the respective figures for males over 17 and people with some higher education were, of course, lower still with 42 per cent and 31 per cent; Gertner 1985: 32A). The drop-off at the age of 30 was also much less dramatic. In 1972, 25–29-year-olds made up 9 per cent of the population over 11, and bought 14 per cent of all tickets purchased by those over 11; the figures for 30–39-year-olds were 15 per cent of the population and 11 per cent of tickets (Jowett 1976: 485). In 1983, the respective figures for 25–29-year-olds were 11 per cent of the population and 14 per cent of tickets, that is, this group bought proportionally fewer tickets than in 1972; for 30–39-year-olds the figure was 18 per cent for both the population share and the share of tickets, which means that this group bought proportionally more tickets than in 1972 (Gertner 1985: 30A). While this trend towards a more inclusive audience was, as we have seen, already under way in the mid-1970s, it is reasonable to assume that the huge impact of family-adventure movies such as *Star Wars* and female-oriented superhits such as *Grease* helped to make cinema audiences ever more inclusive from 1977 onwards. This ties in with the supposition that the family-adventures and women's pictures among the superhits owed their breakaway success precisely to attracting those people who rarely, if ever, went to the cinema, whereas many of the New Hollywood superhits depended largely on (repeat) attendance by young people who tended to be frequent cinemagoers. Where several of the New Hollywood superhits further alienated those who only rarely attended cinemas (especially older people and women), most of the superhits of 1977–86 signalled to the American population that it was safe to go to the movies again (see also Krämer 1998b, 2002b, 2004, 2006).

From this analysis, the years 1967–76 do indeed emerge as a very distinctive period in American film history. Despite all its commercial and critical successes, American cinema from 1967 to 1976 was, as far as its stories were concerned, highly derivative (with most superhits adapting stories from other media), and it was quite exclusive, insofar as it failed to attract large segments of the American population, instead primarily serving male youth. What *Star Wars* and similar breakaway hits from 1977 onwards achieved was to bring back many people who had previously given up on the cinema, and also to generate new stories (based on long-established traditions, of course, but never told before) which were so appealing that they have been extended and re-told countless times both in films and in other media ever since. Rather than primarily adapting existing stories for a niche cinema audience of male youth, since the late 1970s movies have once again become a genuine mass medium, and an important driving force in the entertainment industry.

In conclusion, then, this book has offered a new perspective on the period 1967–76 in American cinema, a decade which saw the theatrical release of over 2000 American-financed films in the US (plus roughly the same amount of foreign-financed films; Finler 2003: 367). From this vast corpus, using an inflation-adjusted box office chart, I selected a small group of breakaway hits, demonstrating the centrality of these films for the film industry and its audiences, and establishing their distinctive thematic concerns by comparing them with the superhits of the decades preceding and following the New Hollywood. This comparison revealed significant thematic shifts between the three sets of superhits, which also could be found across the annual top ten lists. Notwithstanding the incredible diversity of the overall output of the American film industry, from the Roadshow Era to the New Hollywood the thematic emphasis of hit movies shifted from key developments in Western history to the social divisions of contemporary America and the operations of its main institutions, from foreign nations and nationalities to American ethnicities and race relations, from family-friendly representations to graphic displays of sex and violence.

I offered an explanation for these thematic shifts by examining the dynamic interplay between the output of the American film industry and the composition and preferences of cinema audiences in the US, which can be approximated with the help of audience surveys conducted at the time. This examination revealed that in the late 1960s and early 1970s overall industry output was in line with some audience preferences (especially those of male youth), but not others. In particular, ongoing preferences for traditional family-oriented musicals and historical epics, which continued to be immensely popular on television and in audience surveys in the 1970s, were no longer serviced in cinemas during the first half of the decade, and the objections of many people to, among other things, high levels of sex and violence were disregarded. As a result, large segments of the American population (notably women and older people) were alienated from the cinemagoing experience, some only temporarily, others permanently. Hence, it is not the case that Hollywood always gives the people what they want. However, ignoring the concerns and preferences of large population segments is clearly detrimental to the industry's long-term financial health, and it could therefore be expected that efforts would soon be made to overcome the alienation of those segments, as indeed they were with increasing success after 1972.

In order to explain Hollywood's bias and the polarised responses of various audience segments in the late 1960s and early 1970s, I examined a number of developments in the American entertainment industry and in American society at large. Assuming, as most film historians do, that there is some relationship between changes in films and changes in society at large, I used opinion polls as a measure of key aspects of social, cultural and political change. I argued that, across the 1960s and 1970s, public opinion in the US became ever more polarised, with youth being at the forefront of liberalisation, and older people often being left behind (although on the whole their attitudes were slowly becoming more liberal as well). The relationship between the thematic concerns of hit movies and the outlook of the increasingly liberal youth audience was by no means straightforward. Hit movies were in line with some liberal attitudes (notably about sex, race, ethnicity, foreign policy and the shortcomings of the social, political and economic order), but ignored, even reversed others (notably about gender equality). Furthermore, it has to be emphasised that for more liberal movies to be made in the first place, the film industry had to change so as to make it more responsive to, and potentially even an engine of, social change. I argued that the integration, or transformation, of film companies into corporations operating across a range of media, and indeed across a range of industries, disrupted their long-established hierarchies and traditional ways of doing business (most notably the implementation of the Production Code). This disruption created opportunities for new generations of film executives and filmmakers, often with a politically and culturally liberal outlook, and for the quick adoption of (thematic) innovations in television, publishing and popular music. The hits of the New Hollywood arose from the interplay between such changes in the film industry and the liberalisation of American society.

Finally, I want to suggest that the integrated analysis of hit patterns, film industrial developments and social change offered in this study with respect to the New Hollywood can be applied to other periods of change in American film history. As this conclusion has demonstrated, another obvious candidate for such an analysis is the transformation of American cinema in the late 1970s. But this requires, I think, another book.

APPENDICES

Appendix 1: Annual Top Ten 1967–1976

A note of caution: When determining annual box office charts, one confronts three major problems. Firstly, a film's run often extends beyond one calendar year; indeed, until the 1970s, many films stayed in cinemas for several years. Secondly, until the 1980s many hit movies had re-releases, sometimes soon after their initial release, sometimes many years later. Thirdly, figures tend to vary slightly from source to source, and what is arguably the most authoritative source, *Variety*, has over the years adjusted its rental figures for particular films in the light of new information. Charts like the ones presented below are therefore only ever an approximation. It is also worth pointing out that when compiling annual charts, some sources use the year when a film was produced rather than the year in which it was actually released into theatres. I have used the latter.

The following listings rank the top ten releases of each year in terms of rental income, that is the money paid by exhibitors to distributors, which is usually about 40–60 per cent of box office gross, that is the money paid by cinemagoers for their tickets. Figures are taken from *Variety*'s 1993 'All-Time Film Rental Champs', which lists all films with rentals of at least $3m in alphabetical order (Cohn 1993: C76–106, 108). A year-by-year breakdown was kindly provided to me by Sheldon Hall.

I had to amend this breakdown in certain instances with the help of the annual box office charts and the annual updates of the all-time chart which *Variety* publishes every year in one of its January issues. According to Lawrence Cohn, *The Aristocats* (1970), *Robin Hood* (1973) and *The Rocky Horror Picture Show* (1975) were among the top-grossing movies of their year of release, but these films earned the vast majority of their rentals during the decades after their initial release and were therefore excluded. For *The Jungle Book* (1967), which earned a lot of money during re-releases in the 1980s and 1990s, and *Gone With the Wind* (1939), which has been re-released numerous times since the 1940s, I have estimated the rentals earned during the decade 1967–76. The estimate for *The Jungle Book* is taken from 'The Top 200 Moneymaking Films of All Time', compiled by *Variety* in January 1979 (reprinted in Steinberg 1980: 4–8). For *Gone With the Wind*, I deducted the rentals the film had earned by the end of 1966 from the figure for the end of 1976 (Anon. 1967b: 21; Anon. 1977: 16). The film earned $36m in rentals during the decade 1967–76, most of it during a re-release in 1967/68, and is therefore listed as one of the top hits of 1967. By the same calculation, *The Sound of Music* (1965) also earned $36m during this decade and *Doctor Zhivago* (1965) $32m. However, most of this money did not derive from re-releases but from the extended run of their original release; therefore I have not listed them in the annual charts for 1967–76.

The top ten lists resulting from these amendments are very similar to those published for the 1970s by David Cook (2000: 497–503). For several films, notably *The Exorcist* (1973), *The Sting* (1973), *Blazing Saddles* (1974) and *Jaws* (1975), the rental figures given below include revenues from re-releases in the late 1970s. Where available, rental figures were complemented with the figures for box office gross, taken from *The Variety Almanac 2000* (*Variety* 2000: 62–7).

It is important to point out that figures are not adjusted for inflation and they cover income from both the US and Canada. All figures are rounded.

1967
1   *The Graduate*, $44m rentals ($105m gross)
2   *Gone With the Wind* re-release, $36m
3   *Guess Who's Coming to Dinner*, $26m
4   *The Jungle Book*, $25m
5   *Bonnie and Clyde*, $23m
6   *The Dirty Dozen*, $20m
7   *The Valley of the Dolls*, $20m

8   *You Only Live Twice*, $19m
9   *To Sir, With Love*, $19m
10 *Thoroughly Modern Millie*, $16m

1968
1   *Funny Girl*, $26m
2   *2001: A Space Odyssey*, $26
3   *The Odd Couple*, $20m
4   *Bullitt*, $19m
5   *Romeo and Juliet*, $17
6   *Oliver!*, $17m
7   *Planet of the Apes*, $15m
7   *Rosemary's Baby*, $15m
9   *Yours, Mine and Ours*, $12m
10 *The Lion in Winter*, $10m

1969
1   *Butch Cassidy and the Sundance Kid*, $46m ($102m gross)
2   *The Love Bug*, $23m
3   *Midnight Cowboy*, $21m
4   *Easy Rider*, $19m
5   *Hello, Dolly!*, $15m
6   *Bob & Carol & Ted & Alice*, $15m
7   *Paint Your Wagon*, $15m
8   *True Grit*, $14m
9   *Cactus Flower*, $12m
10 *Goodbye, Columbus*, $11m

1970
1   *Love Story*, $49m ($106m gross)
2   *Airport*, $45m (c. $80m gross)
3   *M*A*S*H*, $37m
4   *Patton*, $28m
5   *Woodstock*, $16m
6   *Little Big Man*, $15m
7   *Ryan's Daughter*, $15m
8   *Tora! Tora! Tora!*, $15m

9   *Catch-22*, $12m
10 *The Owl and the Pussycat*, $12m

1971
1   *Fiddler on the Roof*, $38m
2   *Billy Jack*, $33m
3   *The French Connection*, $26m
4   *Summer of '42*, $21m
5   *Diamonds Are Forever*, $20m
6   *Dirty Harry*, $18m
7   *A Clockwork Orange*, $17m
8   *Carnal Knowledge*, $14m
9   *The Last Picture Show*, $13m
10 *Bedknobs and Broomsticks*, $11m

1972
1   *The Godfather*, $87m ($135m gross)
2   *The Poseidon Adventure*, $42m ($85m gross)
3   *What's Up, Doc?*, $28m
4   *Deliverance*, $23m
5   *Jeremiah Johnson*, $22m
6   *Cabaret*, $20m
7   *Deep Throat*, $20m
8   *The Getaway*, $18m
9   *Brother of the Wind*, $12m
10 *Lady Sings the Blues*, $10m

1973
1   *The Exorcist*, $89m ($165m gross)
2   *The Sting*, $78m ($156m gross)
3   *American Graffiti*, $55m ($115m gross)
4   *Papillon*, $23m
5   *The Way We Were*, $22m
6   *Magnum Force*, $20m
7   *Last Tango in Paris*, $17m
8   *Paper Moon*, $17m
9   *Live and Let Die*, $16m

10   *The Devil in Miss Jones*, $15m

1974
1   *The Towering Inferno*, $49m ($116m gross)
2   *Blazing Saddles*, $48m ($120m gross)
3   *Young Frankenstein*, $39m
4   *Earthquake*, $36m
5   *The Trial of Billy Jack*, $31m
6   *The Godfather, Part II*, $31m
7   *Airport 1975*, $25m
8   *The Longest Yard*, $23m
9   *Murder on the Orient Express*, $19m
10   *Herbie Rides Again*, $17m

1975
1   *Jaws*, $130m ($260m gross)
2   *One Flew Over the Cuckoo's Nest*, $60m ($112m gross)
3   *Shampoo*, $24m
4   *Dog Day Afternoon*, $23m
5   *The Life and Times of Grizzly Adams*, $22m
6   *The Return of the Pink Panther*, $20m
7   *Three Days of the Condor*, $20m
8   *Funny Lady*, $19m
9   *The Other Side of the Mountain*, $18m
10   *Tommy*, $18m

1976
1   *Rocky*, $57m ($117m gross)
2   *A Star is Born*, $37m
3   *King Kong*, $37m
4   *Silver Streak*, $30m
5   *All the President's Men*, $30m
6   *The Omen*, $29m
7   *The Bad News Bears*, $25m
8   *The Enforcer*, $24m
9   *In Search of Noah's Ark*, $24m
10   *Midway*, $22m

Appendix 2: Inflation-Adjusted Top 14 of 1967–76

The following chart is based on a Box Office Mojo website (http://www.
boxofficemojo.com/alltime/adjusted.htm; accessed 23 March 2003). This
website attempts to adjust film grosses to average 2002 ticket prices. The
figures for unadjusted grosses used as the basis for this calculation sometimes differ from those in *The Variety Almanac* which were employed in
appendix 1, but this difference does not affect the overall picture (see the
adjusted list in *Variety* 2000: 71). According to Box Office Mojo, *The Jungle
Book* should be included in the Top 14, but, as noted before, the film made
most of its money after 1976 and is therefore excluded. If one were to adjust
the earnings of its re-releases in 1967/68 and 1971/72, *Gone With the Wind*
might just make it into the Top 14. In the all-time inflation-adjusted chart,
the Top 14 for 1967–76 are ranked between no. 7 and no. 63; *Gone With the
Wind* is at no. 1 (with all its releases since 1939 being counted).

1   *Jaws* (1975)
2   *The Exorcist* (1973)
3   *The Sting* (1973)
4   *The Graduate* (1967)
5   *The Godfather* (1972)
6   *Butch Cassidy and the Sundance Kid* (1969)
7   *Love Story* (1970)
8   *Airport* (1970)
9   *American Graffiti* (1973)
10 *Blazing Saddles* (1974)
11 *The Towering Inferno* (1974)
12 *Rocky* (1976)
13 *The Poseidon Adventure* (1972)
14 *One Flew Over the Cuckoo's Nest* (1975)

Appendix 3: Annual Top Five, 1949–66

As in appendix 1, the following listings are based on Sheldon Hall's year-by-year breakdown of *Variety*'s 1993 'All-Time Film Rental Champs' (Cohn 1993: C76–106, 108). Once again, I had to amend this breakdown in certain instances. According to Cohn, the Disney films *Alice in Wonderland* (1951), *Sleeping Beauty* (1959), *Darby O'Gill and the Little People* (1959), *One Hundred and One Dalmatians* (1961), *In Search of the Castaways* (1962), *The Sword in the Stone* (1963) and *That Darn Cat* (1965) as well as *Rear Window* (1954) were among the top-grossing films of their years of release, but they earned a substantial share and in several cases the majority of their rentals in re-releases after 1966 and were therefore excluded. The rental figures used below for Disney's *Cinderella* (1950), *Peter Pan* (1953), *20,000 Leagues Under the Sea* (1954), *Lady and the Tramp* (1955), *Old Yeller* (1957), *The Shaggy Dog* (1959), *Swiss Family Robinson* (1960), *The Parent Trap* (1961), *The Absent-Minded Professor* (1961), *Son of Flubber* (1963) and *Mary Poppins* (1964) exclude all earnings after 1966 (see Anon. 1967b). However, several roadshows, most notably *The Sound of Music* (1965) and *Doctor Zhivago* (1965), had extended runs into the late 1960s as well as re-releases in the early 1970s; I have included revenues from these extended runs and re-releases in the figures given below.

The figures are not adjusted for inflation and they cover income from both the US and Canada. All figures are rounded.

1949
1   *Samson and Delilah*, $12m rentals
2   *Battleground*, $5m
3   *Jolson Sings Again*, $5m
4   *Sands of Iwo Jima*, $5m
5   *I Was a Male War Bride*, $4m

1950
1   *Cinderella*, $9m
2   *King Solomon's Mines*, $6m
3   *Annie Get Your Gun*, $5m
4   *Cheaper By the Dozen*, $4m
5   *Born Yesterday*, $4m

1951

1   *Quo Vadis*, $12m
2   *Show Boat*, $6m
3   *David and Bathsheba*, $5m
4   *The Great Caruso*, $5m
5   *A Streetcar Named Desire*, $4m

1952

1   *This is Cinerama*, $15m
2   *The Greatest Show on Earth*, $14m
3   *The Snows of Kilimanjaro*, $7m
4   *Ivanhoe*, $6m
5   *Hans Christian Andersen*, $6m

1953

1   *The Robe*, $18m
2   *From Here to Eternity*, $12m
3   *Shane*, $8m
4   *How to Marry a Millionaire*, $7m
5   *Peter Pan*, $7m

1954

1   *White Christmas*, $12m
2   *The Caine Mutiny*, $9m
3   *20,000 Leagues Under the Sea*, $9m
4   *The Glenn Miller Story*, $8m
5   *The Country Girl*, $7m

1955

1   *Cinerama Holiday*, $12m
2   *Mister Roberts*, $9m
3   *Lady and the Tramp*, $8m
4   *Battle Cry*, $8m
5   *Oklahoma!*,$7m

1956

1   *The Ten Commandments*, $43m

2   *Around the World in Eighty Days*, $23m
3   *Giant*, $14m
4   *Seven Wonders of the World*, $13m
5   *The King and I*, $9m

1957

1   *The Bridge on the River Kwai*, $17m
2   *Peyton Place*, $12m
3   *Sayonara*, $11m
4   *Old Yeller*, $8m
5   *Raintree County*, $6m

1958

1   *South Pacific*, $18m
2   *Auntie Mame*, $9m
3   *Cat on a Hot Tin Roof*, $9m
4   *No Time for Sergeants*, $9m
5   *Gigi*, $7m

1959

1   *Ben-Hur*, $37m
2   *The Shaggy Dog*, $10m
3   *Operation Petticoat*, $9m
4   *Some Like It Hot*, $8m
5   *Pillow Talk*, $8m

1960

1   *Spartacus*, $10m
2   *Psycho*, $9
3   *Exodus*, $8m
4   *The Alamo*, $8m
5   *Swiss Family Robinson*, $8m

1961

1   *West Side Story*, $20m
2   *The Guns of Navarone*, $13m
3   *El Cid*, $12m

4 *The Parent Trap*, $9m

5 *The Absent-Minded Professor*, $9m

1962

1 *How the West Was Won*, $21m

2 *The Longest Day*, $18m

3 *Lawrence of Arabia*, $17

4 *The Music Man*, $8m

5 *That Touch of Mink*, $8m

1963

1 *Cleopatra*, $26m

2 *It's a Mad, Mad, Mad, Mad World*, $21m

3 *Tom Jones*, $17m

4 *Irma la Douce*, $12m

5 *Son of Flubber*, $7m

1964

1 *My Fair Lady*, $34m

2 *Mary Poppins*, $31m

3 *Goldfinger*, $23m

4 *The Carpetbaggers*, $16m

5 *From Russia With Love*, $10m

1965

1 *The Sound of Music*, $80m

2 *Doctor Zhivago*, $47m

3 *Thunderball*, $29m

4 *Those Magnificent Men in Their Flying Machines*, $14m

5 *The Great Race*, $11m

1966

1 *Hawaii*, $16m

2 *The Bible: In the Beginning*, $15m

3 *Who's Afraid of Virginia Woolf?*, $15m

4 *The Sand Pebbles*, $14m

5 *A Man for All Seasons*, $13m

Appendix 4: Inflation-Adjusted Top 14 of 1949–66

The following chart is again based on the Box Office Mojo website (http://
www.boxofficemojo.com/alltime/adjusted.htm; accessed 23 March 2003).
According to Box Office Mojo, *One Hundred and One Dalmatians* (1961)
and *Sleeping Beauty* (1959) are in the Top 14, but these films made most
of their money after 1966 and are therefore excluded. I have also excluded
Let's Make Love (1960) because its presence on the Box Office Mojo list is
at odds with information about this film's box office performance from all
other sources.

The ranking for *Mary Poppins* is probably too high, due to the inclusion of revenues generated by re-releases after 1966, and *My Fair Lady* is
ranked unexpectedly low, which is probably due to ongoing disagreements
about the film's earnings. Judging by the rental figures given in appendix
3, both *This Is Cinerama* and *South Pacific* should be included in the Top
14, but it is possible that their box office grosses, which form the basis for
the inflation adjustments, were comparatively low (because the distributor
was able to demand a larger share of box office revenues). In the all-time
inflation-adjusted chart, the Top 14 of 1949–66 are ranked between no. 3
and no. 67.

1   *The Sound of Music* (1965)
2   *The Ten Commandments* (1956)
3   *Doctor Zhivago* (1965)
4   *Ben-Hur* (1959)
5   *Mary Poppins* (1964)
6   *Thunderball* (1965)
7   *Cleopatra* (1963)
8   *Goldfinger* (1964)
9   *The Robe* (1953)
10 *Around the World in Eighty Days* (1956)
11 *The Greatest Show on Earth* (1952)
12 *My Fair Lady* (1964)
13 *West Side Story* (1961)
14 *The Bridge on the River Kwai* (1957)

Appendix 5: Inflation-Adjusted Top 14 of 1977–86

The following chart is once again based on the Box Office Mojo website (http://www.boxofficemojo.com/alltime/adjusted.htm; accessed 23 March 2003). Curiously, *Saturday Night Fever* is absent from this chart, despite the fact that its $139m gross is higher than the grosses for *Superman* and *Smokey and the Bandit* (*Variety* 2000: 64). In the all-time inflation-adjusted chart, the Top 14 of 1977–86 are ranked between no. 2 and no. 60.

1 *Star Wars* (1977)
2 *E.T. The Extra-Terrestrial* (1982)
3 *The Empire Strikes Back* (1980)
4 *Return of the Jedi* (1983)
5 *Raiders of the Lost Ark* (1981)
6 *Grease* (1978)
7 *Ghostbusters* (1984)
8 *Bevery Hills Cop* (1984)
9 *National Lampoon's Animal House* (1978)
10 *Back to the Future* (1985)
11 *Superman* (1978)
12 *Smokey and the Bandit* (1977)
13 *Tootsie* (1982)
14 *Close Encounters of the Third Kind* (1977)

BIBLIOGRAPHY

Allen, Michael (2003) *Contemporary US Cinema*. London: Longman.

Alpert, Hollis (1971 [1968]) *'The Graduate* Makes Out', in Arthur F. McClure (ed.) *The Movies: An American Idiom*. Rutherford, Fairleigh Dickinson University Press, 404–10.

Altman, Rick (1999) *Film/Genre*. London: British Film Institute.

Alvey, Mark (2004) '"Too Many Kids and Old Ladies": Quality Demographics and 1960s US Television', *Screen*, 45, 1, 40–62.

Anon. (1962) 'A Family Movie', *Christian Science Monitor*, 19 September.

____ (1963) 'American Audience Preferences Listed at Aspen by Mrs. Twyman', *Boxoffice*, 9 September.

____ (1964) 'Young Finds Audience's Tastes are Against Filth', *Hollywood Reporter*, 16 June.

____ (1965a) 'Film of the Year', *Daily Telegraph*, 28 December.

____ (1965b) 'Feature Pix on TV Watched By 90.7% of Teen-Age Girls', *Hollywood Reporter*, 22 March.

____ (1967a) *'McCall's* Reports a "Sex Backlash"', *Variety*, 19 April.

____ (1967b) 'All-Time Boxoffice Champs', *Variety*, 4 January, 9, 23, 31.

____ (1968a) 'Better Education Big Boon To Film Attendance – Valenti', *Daily Variety*, 2 February.

____ (1968b) 'Valenti Predicts Increased Attendance Based on Research by MPAA', *Boxoffice*, 29 January.

____ (1970) 'Nostalgia Book Club Member Survey: All-Time Favorites', clipping in 'Surveys (1970–1979)' file, Centre for Motion Picture Study, Academy of Motion Picture Arts and Sciences, Beverly Hills (AMPAS).

_____ (1973) 'The Sting is All Pros Playing as Fun-Loving Cons', San Diego Evening Tribune, 20 December.

_____ (1974a) 'Anybody Surprised?', Variety, 28 August.

_____ (1974b) 'Motivational Research in Promotion', Variety, 26 June.

_____ (1974c) 'Survey Says Women Pick Most Motion Picture Fare', Boxoffice, 14 October.

_____ (1974d) Review of Earthquake, Boxoffice, 18 November.

_____ (1974e) Review of Earthquake, Hollywood Reporter, 13 November.

_____ (1977) 'All-Time Film Rental Champs', Variety, 5 January.

_____ (1991a) 'Pix from Afar: National Bests in the US', Variety, 7 January.

_____ (1991b) 'The 1980s: A Reference Guide to Motion Pictures, Television, VCR, and Cable', The Velvet Light Trap, 27, 77–88.

Barker, Martin (2004) 'Violence Redux', in Steven Jay Schneider (ed.) New Hollywood Violence. Manchester: Manchester University Press, 57–79.

Basinger, Jeanine (1986) The World War II Combat Film: Anatomy of a Genre. New York: Columbia University Press.

Belton, John (1992) Widescreen Cinema. Cambridge, MA: Harvard University Press.

Bernardoni, James (1991) The New Hollywood: What the Movies Did with the New Freedoms of the Seventies. Jefferson: McFarland.

Biskind, Peter (1998) Easy Riders, Raging Bulls: How the Sex-Drugs-and-Rock 'n' Roll Generation Saved Hollywood. New York: Simon and Schuster.

Black, Gregory D. (1998) The Catholic Crusade Against the Movies, 1940–1975. Cambridge: Cambridge University Press.

Bogle, Donald (1997) Toms, Coons, Mulattoes, Mammies, and Bucks: An Interpretive History of Blacks in American Films (third edition). New York: Continuum.

Brownstein, Ronald (1992) The Power and the Glitter: The Hollywood-Washington Connection. New York: Vintage.

Burns, Gary (1983) 'Trends in Lyrics in the Annual Top Twenty Songs in the United States, 1963–1972', Popular Music and Society, 9, 1, 25–39.

Champlin, Charles (1970a) 'Love Story Tells It Like It Always Was', Los Angeles Times, 20 December, Calendar, 1, 20.

_____ (1970b) 'Airport Recalls Older Hollywood', Los Angeles Times, 4 March.

Cohn, Lawrence (1993) 'All-Time Film Rental Champs', Variety, 10 May, C76–106, 108.

Cook, David A. (2000) Lost Illusions: American Cinema in the Shadow of Watergate and Vietnam, 1970–1979. New York: Scribner's.

Crist, Judith (1991) *Take 22: Moviemakers on Moviemaking* (expanded edition). New York: Continuum.

Cross, Gary (1997) *Kids' Stuff: Toys and the Changing World of American Childhood.* Cambridge, MA: Harvard University Press.

Denisoff, R. Serge and William D. Romanowski (eds) (1991) *Risky Business: Rock in Film.* New Brunswick: Transaction.

De Vany, Arthur (2004) *Hollywood Economics: How Extreme Uncertainty Shapes the Film Industry.* London: Routledge.

Dorr, John H. (1974) Review of *The Towering Inferno, Hollywood Reporter,* 16 December.

Earnest, Olen J. (1985) '*Star Wars*: A Case Study in Motion Picture Marketing', *Current Research in Film,* 1, 1–18.

Elley, Derek (ed.) (2000) *Variety Movie Guide 2000.* New York: Perigee.

Elsaesser, Thomas, Alexander Horwath and Noel King (eds) (2004) *The Last Great American Picture Show: New Hollywood Cinema in the 1970s.* Amsterdam: Amsterdam University Press.

Erens, Patricia (1984) *The Jew in American Cinema.* Bloomington: Indiana University Press.

Finler, Joel W. (1988) *The Hollywood Story.* London: Octopus.

_____ (2003) *The Hollywood Story* (third edition). London: Wallflower Press.

Gabler, Neal (1989) *An Empire of Their Own: How the Jews Invented Hollywood.* London: W. H. Allen.

Garncarz, Joseph (1994) 'Hollywood in Germany: The Role of American Films in Germany, 1925–1990', in David W. Ellwood and Rob Kroes (eds) *Hollywood in Europe: Experiences of a Cultural Hegemony.* Amsterdam: VU University Press, 122–35.

_____ (1996) *Populäres Kino in Deutschland: Internationalisierung einer Filmkultur, 1925–1990.* Unpublished post-doctoral dissertation, University of Cologne.

Gelmis, Joseph (1971) *The Film Director as Superstar.* London: Secker & Warburg.

Gertner, Richard (ed.) (1978) *International Motion Picture Almanac.* New York: Quigley.

_____ (ed.) (1985) *International Motion Picture Almanac.* New York: Quigley.

Gilbert, Toni (1970) Review of *Love Story, Entertainment World,* 20 Feburary.

Gilbey, Ryan (2003) *It Don't Worry Me: Nashville, Jaws, Star Wars and Beyond.* London: Faber and Faber.

Greene, Eric (1998) *Planet of the Apes as American Myth: Race, Politics, and Popular Culture.* Hanover: Wesleyan University Press.

Gropenwaldt, Raoul (1972) 'At Last – Good Family Film', *Evening Outlook*, 14 December.

Hackett, Alice Payne and James Henry Burke (1977) *80 Years of Best Sellers, 1895–1975*. New York: R. R. Bowker.

Haines, Richard W. (2003) *The Moviegoing Experience, 1968–2001*. Jefferson: McFarland.

Hall, Sheldon (1999) *Hard Ticket Giants: Hollywood Blockbusters in the Widescreen Era*. Two volumes. Unpublished PhD dissertation, University of East Anglia.

____ (2002) 'Tall Revenue Features: The Genealogy of the Modern Blockbuster', in Steve Neale (ed.) *Genre and Contemporary Hollywood*. London: British Film Institute, 11–26.

Hilmes, Michele (1990) 'Pay Television: Breaking the Broadcast Bottleneck', in Tino Balio (ed.) *Hollywood in the Age of Television*. Boston: Unwin Hyman, 297–318.

Hoberman, J. (1998) '"A Test for the Individual Viewer": *Bonnie and Clyde*'s Violent Reception', in Jeffrey H. Goldstein (ed.) *Why We Watch: The Attractions of Violent Entertainment*. New York: Oxford University Press, 116–43

____ (2003) *The Dream Life: Movies, Media, and the Mythology of the Sixties*. New York: New Press.

Isserman, Maurice and Michael Kazin (2004) *America Divided: The Civil War of the 1960s* (second edition). New York: Oxford University Press.

Jacobs, Diane (1977) *Hollywood Renaissance*. South Brunswick: Barnes.

Jamgocyan, Nik (1998) 'Big Boat, Small Screen', *Screen International*, 26 June, 9.

Jarvie, Ian C. (1990) 'Stars and Ethnicity: Hollywood and the United States, 1932–51', in Lester D. Friedman (ed.) *Unspeakable Images: Ethnicity and the American Cinema*. Champaign: University of Illinois Press, 82–111.

Jenkins, Henry (1992) *Textual Poachers: Television Fans and Participatory Culture*. New York: Routledge.

Jowett, Garth (1976) *Film: The Democratic Art*. Boston: Little, Brown.

____ (1996) '"A Significant Medium for the Communication of Ideas": The Miracle Decision and the Decline of Motion Picture Censorship', in Francis G. Couvares (ed.) *Movie Censorship and American Culture*. Washington, DC: Smithsonian Institution Press, 258-76.

Kanfer, Stefan (1970) 'The Love Bug', *Time*, 21 December.

____ (1971 [1967]) 'The Shock of Freedom in Films', in Arthur F. McClure (ed.) *The Movies: An American Idiom*. Rutherford: Fairleigh Dickinson University Press, 322–33.

Kindem, Gorham (1994) *The Live Television Generation of Hollywood Film Directors*. Jefferson: McFarland.

King, Geoff (2002) *New Hollywood Cinema: An Introduction*. London: I. B. Tauris.

Knight, Arthur (1971) 'Author, Author', *Saturday Review*, 2 January.

Kolker, Robert (1980) *A Cinema of Loneliness: Penn, Kubrick, Coppola, Scorsese, Altman*. Oxford: Oxford University Press.

____ (2000) *A Cinema of Loneliness: Penn, Stone, Kubrick, Scorsese, Spielberg, Altman* (third revised edition). Oxford: Oxford University Press.

Koszarski, Richard (ed.) *Hollywood Directors, 1941–1976*. New York: Oxford University Press.

Krämer, Peter (1998a) 'Post-Classical Hollywood', in John Hill and Pamela Church Gibson (eds) *The Oxford Guide to Film Studies*. Oxford: Oxford University Press, 289–309.

____ (1998b) 'Would You Take Your Child To See This Film? The Cultural and Social Work of the Family-Adventure Movie', in Steve Neale and Murray Smith (eds) *Contemporary Hollywood Cinema*. London: Routledge, 294–311.

____ (1999) 'A Powerful Cinema-going Force? Hollywood and Female Audiences since the 1960s', in Melvyn Stokes and Richard Maltby (eds) *Identifying Hollywood's Audiences: Cultural Identity and the Movies*. London: British Film Institute, 98–112.

____ (2000) '"Faith in relations between people": Audrey Hepburn, *Roman Holiday* and European Integration', in Diana Holmes and Alison Smith (eds) *100 Years of European Cinema: Entertainment or Ideology?* Manchester: Manchester University Press, 195–206.

____ (2002a) 'Hollywood in Germany/Germany in Hollywood', in Tim Bergfelder, Erica Carter and Deniz Göktürk (eds) *The German Cinema Book*. London: British Film Institute, 227–37.

____ (2002b) '"The best Disney film Disney never made': Children's Films and the Family Audience in American Cinema Since the 1960s', in Steve Neale (ed.) *Genre and Contemporary Hollywood*. London: British Film Institute, 183–98.

____ (2004) '"It's aimed at kids – the kid in everybody": George Lucas, *Star Wars* and Children's Entertainment', in Yvonne Tasker (ed.) *Action and Adventure Cinema*. London: Routledge, 358-70.

____ (2006) 'Big Pictures: Studying Contemporary Hollywood Cinema Through its Greatest Hits', *Screen Methods: Comparative Readings in Film Studies*. London: Wallflower Press, 124–32.

Ladd, Everett Carll and Karlyn H. Bowman (1998) *What's Wrong: A Survey of*

American Satisfaction and Complaint. Washington, DC: The AEI Press.

Lafferty, William (1990) 'Feature Films on Prime-Time Television', in Tino Balio (ed.) *Hollywood in the Age of Television*. Boston: Unwin Hyman, 235–56.

Leff, Leonard J. and Jerold L. Simmons (1990) *The Dame in the Kimono: Hollywood, Censorship, and the Production Code from the 1920s to the 1960s*. New York: Grove Weidenfeld.

Lev, Peter (2000) *American Films of the 70s: Conflicting Visions*. Austin: University of Texas Press.

Levy, Emanuel (1989) 'The Democratic Elite: America's Movie Stars', *Qualitative Sociology*, 12, 1, 28–54.

Lewis, Jerry (1972) 'Children, Too Have Film Rights', *Variety*, 5 January, 32.

Lewis, Jon (ed.) (1998) *The New American Cinema*. Durham: Duke University Press.

____ (2000) *Hollywood v. Hardcore: How the Struggle over Censorship Saved the Modern Film Industry*. New York: New York University Press.

Long, Elizabeth (1985) *The American Dream and the Popular Novel*. Boston: Routledge and Kegan Paul.

Man, Glen (1994) *Radical Visions: American Film Renaissance, 1967–1976*. Westport: Greenwood.

May, Lary (2000) *The Big Tomorrow: Hollywood and the Politics of the American Way*. Chicago: University of Chicago Press.

Mayer, William G. (1993) *The Changing American Mind: How and Why American Public Opinion Changed between 1960 and 1988*. Ann Arbor: University of Michigan Press.

Meade, James (1973) '*The Sting*: Entertainment', *San Diego Union*, 23 December.

Miller, Stephen Paul (1999) *The Seventies Now: Culture as Surveillance*. Durham: Duke University Press.

Monaco, Paul (2001) *The Sixties, 1960–1969*. New York: Scribner's.

Moser, James D. (ed.) (1997) *International Motion Picture Almanac*. New York: Quigley.

Mott, Frank Luther (1947) *Golden Multitudes: The Story of Best Sellers in the United States*. New York: Macmillan.

Neale, Steve (2000) *Genre and Hollywood*. London: Routledge.

____ (2003) 'Hollywood Blockbusters: Historical Dimensions', in Julian Stringer (ed.) *Movie Blockbusters*. London: Routledge, 47–60.

Neale, Steve and Murray Smith (eds) (1998) *Contemporary Hollywood Cinema*. London: Routledge.

Newspaper Advertising Bureau (1974) 'Movie Going and Leisure Time', folder MFL x n.c. 2,101, 4, Performing Arts Research Center, New York Public Library.

Ozersky, Josh (2003) *Archie Bunker's America: TV in an Era of Change, 1968–1978.* Carbondale: Southern Illinois University Press.

People (2000) *2001 People Entertainment Almanac.* New York: Cader Books.

Perry, George (1998) *Steven Spielberg.* London: Orion.

Pleck, Elizabeth H. (2000) *Celebrating the Family: Ethnicity, Consumer Culture and Family Rituals.* Cambridge: Harvard University Press.

Powers, Stephen, David J. Rothman and Stanley Rothman (1996) *Hollywood's America: Social and Political Themes in Motion Pictures.* Boulder: Westview.

Prince, Stephen (1998) *Savage Cinema: Sam Peckinpah and the Rise of Ultraviolent Movies.* London: Athlone.

____ (ed.) (2000a) *Screening Violence.* New Brunswick: Rutgers University Press.

____ (2000b) *A New Pot of Gold: Hollywood Under the Electronic Rainbow, 1980–1989.* Berkeley: University of California Press.

____ (2003) *Classical Film Violence: Designing and Regulating Brutality in Hollywood Cinema, 1930–1968.* New Brunswick: Rutgers University Press.

Ray, Robert B. (1985) *A Certain Tendency of the Hollywood Cinema, 1930–1980.* Princeton: Princeton University Press.

Roddick, Nick (1980) 'Only the Stars Survive: Disaster Movies in the Seventies', in David Bradby, Louis James and Bernard Sharrett (eds) *Performance and Politics in Popular Cinema.* Cambridge: Cambridge University Press, 243–69.

Ryan, Michael and Douglas Kellner (1988) *Camera Politica: The Politics and Ideology of Contemporary Hollywood Film.* Bloomington: Indiana University Press.

Salewicz, Chris (1998) *George Lucas.* London: Orion.

Schatz, Thomas (1993) 'The New Hollywood', in Jim Collins, Hilary Radner and Ava Preacher Collins (eds) *Film Theory Goes to the Movies.* New York: Routledge, 8–36.

Scott, Vernon (1970) 'Universal Appears to Have a Winner in its *Airport*', *Hollywood Citizen-News*, 18 February.

____ (1972) '*Poseidon*: Hollywood's Movie Movie', *Los Angeles Herald-Examiner*, 26 December.

Seventeen (1967) 'Movie Survey', January, press release contained in 'Surveys 1960–1969' folder, AMPAS.

Shone, Tom (2004) *Blockbuster: How Hollywood Learned to Stop Worrying and Love the Summer.* London: Simon and Schuster.

Simon, John (1968) 'Nulla Cum Laude', *The New Leader*, 26 February, 30–1.

Simonet, Thomas (1987) 'Conglomerates and Content: Remakes, Sequels, and Series in the New Hollywood', *Current Research in Film*, 3, 154–62.

Smith, Greg (1998) *The Sounds of Commerce: Marketing Popular Film Music*. New York: Columbia University Press.

Sobchak, Vivian (1990) '"Surge and Splendor": A Phenomenology of the Hollywood Historical Epic', *Representations*, 29, 24–49.

Steinberg, Cobbett S. (1980) *Film Facts*. New York: Facts on File.

Stempel, Tom (2001) *American Audiences on Movies and Moviegoing*. Lexington: University Press of Kentucky.

Thompson, Kristin (1999) *Storytelling in the New Hollywood: Understanding Classical Narrative Technique*. Cambridge, MA: Harvard University Press.

Variety (2000) *The Variety Almanac 2000*. London: Boxtree.

Walsh, Frank (1996) *Sin and Censorship: The Catholic Church and the Motion Picture Industry*. New Haven: Yale University Press.

Warga, Wayne (1968) 'Facts of Life About Movie Audiences', *Los Angeles Times*, 29 December, Calendar 1, 14.

Wasser, Frederick (2001) *Veni, Vidi, Video: The Hollywood Empire and the VCR*. Austin: University of Texas Press.

Wattenberg, Ben J. (ed.) (1976) *The Statistical History of the United States*. New York: Basic Books.

Wilson, Christopher P. (2000) *Cop Knowledge: Police Power and Cultural Narrative in Twentieth-Century America*. Chicago: University of Chicago Press.

Wolf, William (1970) 'Poll of Moviegoers Uncorks Surprises', *Entertainment World*, 27 January, 7.

Wood, Robin (1986) *Hollywood From Vietnam to Reagan*. New York: Columbia University Press.

_____ (2003) *Hollywood From Vietnam to Reagan ... and Beyond*. New York: Columbia University Press.

Yankelovich, Daniel (1974) *The New Morality: A Profile of American Youth in the 70s*. New York: McGraw-Hill.

INDEX

The Hollywood Story
Joel W. Finler

2003

452 pages

1-903364-66-3   £18.99 (pbk)

Hollywood is synonymous with American cinema. Powerful moguls, beautiful stars, art and commerce, extremes of success and failure – all are encapsulated in the name of the small district northwest of Los Angeles that became the centre of the movie-making world.

In *The Hollywood Story*, Joel W. Finler explores the history of the American movie industry from the silent era up to the present day. In individual chapters that cover each of the major studios, the author considers the key actors, directors and frequently overlooked technicians who contributed to filmmaking history. The book includes a wealth of information on the development of colour, wide-screen processes and the transition from silent cinema to sound. Additionally, Joel W. Finler has compiled an unrivalled amount of financial information which is presented in simple graphs and tables, making it clearer than ever just what, and who, are the big winners and losers in Hollywood.

The Hollywood Story won the British Film Institute award as the outstanding film book of 1989. This fully revised and updated edition brings the facts and figures into the new millennium and includes an entirely new chapter on the studio that emerged in the 1990s as one of the most powerful of all – Disney.

Joel W. Finler has worked as a writer and lecturer on cinema and as a film critic for *Time Out*. He is the author of numerous books about cinema including *All Time Movie Greats* (1975), *The Movie Directors Story* (1985) and several works on directors such as Alfred Hitchcock and Erich von Stroheim.

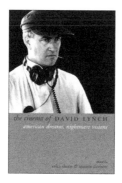

The Cinema of David Lynch
American Dreams, Nightmare Visions

Edited by Erica Sheen and
Annette Davison

2004
208 pages
1-903364-85-X   £15.99 (pbk)
1-903364-86-8   £45.00 (hbk)

David Lynch is an anomaly. A pioneer of the American 'indie' aesthetic, he also
works in Hollywood and for network television. He has created some of the most
disturbing images in contemporary cinema, and produced startlingly innovative
work in sound. This collection offers a range of theoretically divergent readings
that demonstrate not only the difficulty of locating interpretative positions
for Lynch's work, but also the pleasure of finding new ways of thinking about
it. Films discussed include *Blue Velvet*, *Wild at Heart*, *The Straight Story* and
Mulholland Drive.

Erica Sheen lectures in literary theory and film at the University of Sheffield,
UK.
Annette Davison Annette Davison lectures in music and film at the University of
Edinburgh, UK.

'The 12 essays in this collection – all written expressly for this volume by film and
media scholars in the US, Europe and Australia – shed light on the director and
his oeuvre. Among the many topics covered are Lynch's use of parody, allegory,
pastiche, music, female performers, and facial close-ups; some contributors
apply psychoanalytical and feminist theories to his work. The result is a highly
readable volume that deserves a place in film literature. Recommended.'
CHOICE

The Cinema of Terrence Malick
Poetic Visions of America

Edited by Hannah Patterson

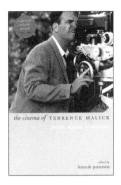

2003

208 pages

1-903364-75-2   £15.99 (pbk)

1-903364-76-0   £45.00 (hbk)

Terrence Malick is one of Hollywood's most enigmatic and legendary film-makers. Despite his limited output, and a famous twenty-year absence from cinema, *Badlands*, *Days of Heaven* and *The Thin Red Line* have challenged notions of contemporary film language. This collection explores issues of identity, the poetics of cinema, representation of the road, youth culture and the American West, the depiction of landscape and nature, use of sound and music, and the influence of philosopher Martin Heidegger. Particular emphasis is placed on *The Thin Red Line*, an important classic of modern cinema.

Hannah Patterson is co-editor of *Contemporary British and Irish Film Directors* (Wallflower Press, 2001) and *Contemporary North American Film Directors* (Wallflower Press, 2002), and a freelance writer.

'Wallflower has published several appetising collections of essays on contemporary auteurs – Lynch, Moretti, Wenders, Lepage etc – but this is not just a fairly exemplary study; it's one of the most useful books on film criticism in a while.'
Geoff Andrew, *Time Out*

'Terrence Malick is a screen poet, an incomparable filmmaker who takes us into the spiritual realm and renews our sense of mystery. This comprehensive study explores his unique vision and illuminates every facet of his work.'
Martin Sheen

Film Noir
From Berlin to Sin City
Mark Bould

2005
144 pages
1-904764-50-9   £12.99 (pbk)

The delectable films that constitute this corpus, featuring hard-boiled men and even harder-boiled women, vertiginous investigations and all manner of entrapment, represent, as Bould's indispensable volume demonstrates ... a cinematic treasure-trove that one can return to, perpetually, with profit and delight.'
– Bob Miklitsch, Ohio University

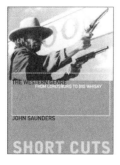

The Western Genre
From Lordsburg to Big Whiskey
John Saunders

2001
144 pages
1-903364-12-4   £12.99 (pbk)

'A clear exposition of the major thematic currents of the genre providing attentive and illuminating reading of major examples.'
– Ed Buscombe, Editor of the *BFI Companion to the Western*

The Horror Genre
From Beelzebub to Blair Witch

Paul Wells

2000

144 pages

1-903364-00-0   £12.99 (pbk)

'An informed and highly readable account that is theoretically broad, benefiting from a wide of cinematic examples … An interesting and accessible overview of the genre.'
– Xavier Mendik, Director of the Cult Film Archive, Brunel University

Science Fiction Cinema
From Outerspace to Cyberspace

Geoff King and Tanya Krzywinska

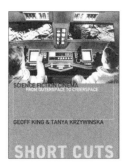

2000

144 pages

1-903364-03-5   £12.99 (pbk)

'The best overview of English-language science-fiction cinema published to date … thorough, clearly written and full of excellent examples. Highly recommended.'
– Steve Neale, Sheffield Hallam University